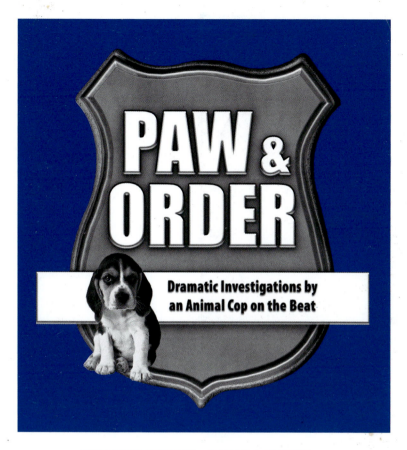

PAW & ORDER

Dramatic Investigations by an Animal Cop on the Beat

ALLISON ESTES • TINA SALAKS

BOWTIE
P R E S S®

Laguna Hills, California

Karla Austin, *Director of Operations & Product Development*
Nick Clemente, *Special Consultant*
Barbara Kimmel, *Editor in Chief*
Amy Stirnkorb, *Designer*

Library of Congress Cataloging-in-Publication Data

Estes, Allison.
   Paw & order : dramatic investigations by an animal cop on the beat /
by Allison Estes and Tina Salaks.
      p. cm.
   ISBN 978-1-933958-21-7
   1. Animal rescue—United States. I. Salaks, Tina. II. Title.
   HV4764.E78 2008
   636.08′32—dc22

                              2007035798

BowTie Press®
A Division of BowTie, Inc.
23172 Plaza Pointe Dr., Ste. 230
Laguna Hills, California 92653

Printed and bound in Singapore
16 15 14 13 12 11 10 09 08   1 2 3 4 5 6 7 8 9 10

Dedication

I've been privileged to know, live with, and work with animals all my life. This book is for all the animals I've loved, especially Boogie, Wednesday, and Cinnamon; and for the humans I live with and love: Luke, Megan, and Kevin. Thanks for putting up with me when I'm writing. And when I'm not.

—*Allison Estes*

This book is dedicated to two incredible, special individuals, and to one extraordinary horse:

My sister, Tami Salaks, whose thoughtfulness, kindness, and gentle spirit touched me deeply and inspires me to this day;

My grandmother, Jenny Salts, who helped foster my love of horses; you didn't drive, but you always managed to find a bus (sometimes three) that would get us to the latest equine event;

My horse Mounty, AKA Thunder; the world always seemed like a better place when I was on your back. Thank you for taking care of me all those years.

—*Tina Salaks*

Contents

Acknowledgments

Several people helped find a home for this book and are deserving of special thanks: Robin Rue at Writers House, for believing in the project, giving it wings, and seeing it through; Art Stickney, who made the dream come true and whose kind and inspirational words about my work I keep on my desktop and read regularly; Barbara Kimmel, our editor at BowTie Press, for keeping *Paw* **in** order and for graciously handling some unexpected chaos; Tony T., for sharing his experiences with and insight into the subculture of animal fighting; and Jill Parsons Stern and Charles Salzberg, for their usual sound and invaluable advice and support.

—*Allison Estes*

A very special thank you to the following people: to Robin Rue, thank you for taking a chance on this book; to the hardworking staff at BowTie Press, and especially Art Stickney and Barbara Kimmel, who are like this book's fairy godparents and whose passion, confidence, and a much welcomed sense of humor have given me a new reason to smile; to Patty Earle, whose enduring friendship and generosity were certainly appreciated during those tough times; to John Galloway, who planted the seed for this book and whose tireless support and encouragement make life so much easier; and to Lisa Lau, for your amazing faith, prayers, and weekly trips to Holy Hill. The following people also deserve a special thank you: my family, Sean and Hilli Dagony-Clark, Andrea Torgovnick, Shannan Carter, Yocheved Berghoff, Kathryn Mellusi, Amy Elliott, Dr. Andrew Lang, Claudine Liberatore, Josephine Pittari, Ray Buttacavoli, Scott Tartar, and Jim Worzala.

—*Tina Salaks*

Introduction

I got to know Tina Salaks while riding a big leopard Appaloosa with blue eyes named Fritz, tailing Tina around Central Park while she was on the job for the Parks Enforcement Patrol (PEP) mounted unit. I was a trainer at Claremont Riding Academy, and the mounted unit had no auxiliary personnel at that time, so sometimes the Claremont instructors would help exercise horses when PEP was short-handed. Tina was so good at the diplomacy of law enforcement and always great with animals, so her move to the ASPCA was the logical next step.

Not long after Tina started at "the A," she began telling me and others about the cases she was seeing. Some of them were tearjerkers, of course, but more were heartwarming, out-rageously weird, or downright hilarious. And all were completely fascinating. More than one person suggested, "You should write a book."

Tina had all these great stories to tell, but, write a book? Recently, she described to me a nightmare she'd had: she had to go back and repeat high school English! Here's where I came in. I had already written several middle-grade and young-adult novels and was between projects. *Paw & Order* is the result of our friendship and our teamwork: in each case, Tina would recount what happened, and I would turn it into a chapter in the book. The stories are based on her recollections and are reproduced as she told them to me, except for certain changes made to protect the identities of people and animals.

Paw & Order was great fun to write; I hope you'll find it even more fun to read!

—*Allison Estes*

I t's almost the end of my shift and I'm hurrying to check out another report of an abandoned dog. I know the area—a bad section of Queens. You wouldn't go there alone, not even in broad daylight, especially not if you're a woman. It'll probably be dark before I get there.

I find the dog, and her two pups, left by their owner on a small uncovered balcony littered with droppings. There's no evidence of food or water. She's thin and weak, probably dehydrated, and her pups are looking undernourished. Slowly I kneel and offer her the back of my hand to sniff.

"Hey, little girl," I say quietly. "How about you come with me and I'll give you a big bowl of puppy chow?" I rub her gently behind the ears and she tolerates it, but looks up at me warily. In her eyes there is hunger and thirst, and pain and distrust, and in spite of all that, a tiny flicker of hope.

In that dog's eyes is the reason I did that job.

I was a special agent for the ASPCA (American Society for the Prevention of Cruelty to Animals) in New York City.

When I began training as a special agent in November 1999, my friends shook their heads. "You're such a softy," they chided me. "You can't even watch a movie where an animal dies without losing it. How are you going to handle a job where you spend your days seeing abused and neglected animals?"

They had a point. I thought long and hard about what it would be like. What I decided was that, although it might be hard seeing animals suffering on a daily basis, at least I'd be in a position to do something about it.

There's nothing easy about investigating animal cruelty. Every day on the job puts your heart through the wringer: you go from despair and anger to hope and great joy. It's a job that brings terrible frustration and enormous rewards. It often put me in danger. It wore me down and lifted me up, and I wouldn't have traded that job for the world—or even a horse.

ASPCA special agents have been on the job since 1866 when Henry Bergh, diplomat, philanthropist, and lover of animals, started the organization "to alleviate pain and suffering in animals." Bergh had witnessed a carriage driver beating his horse and had stepped in to stop the man. The incident prompted him to found the ASPCA. Modeled after the Royal Society for the Prevention of Cruelty to Animals in England, it was the first such agency in the United States, and it caused quite a stir at its inception, as it has at different times throughout its history.

Those early ASPCA agents, called Berghsmen, carried guns before the New York City police did. The guns were mostly used for shooting critically injured horses and rabid dogs. The ASPCA began using the first ambulance in the country, for horses, two years before the first ambulances for humans were put into service. Bergh, who died in 1888 at age seventy-six, spent his last twenty years patrolling the streets of New York in search of animals in need. While carrying out his mission to

There's nothing easy about investigating animal cruelty. Every day on the job puts your heart through the wringer: you go from despair and anger to hope and great joy. It's a job that brings terrible frustration and enormous rewards. It often put me in danger. It wore me down and lifted me up, and I wouldn't have traded that job for the world—or even a horse.

help animals, he also found the time and means to help establish the New York Society for the Prevention of Cruelty to Children (SPCC).

Contrary to what most people think, the ASPCA is not a national organization. It is a nonprofit organization, completely funded by donations, and it has jurisdiction solely in the state of New York. Other states, cities, and counties have SPCAs (societies for the prevention of cruelty to animals) but these are independent agencies and are not affiliated with the ASPCA.

The organization's function has changed somewhat through the years. A lot of people think the special agents are just "puppy police," but the fact is they stopped catching dogs in 1994. The

ASPCA no longer euthanizes animals, rescues cats stuck in trees, or runs the city's shelters. Another city agency, New York City Animal Care and Control (NYCAC&C), handles these jobs.

The sole function of the Humane Law Enforcement (HLE) department is to investigate reports of cruelty to animals. HLE special agents have full police powers and are able to make their own arrests. The ASPCA is not affiliated with the New York Police Department (NYPD), although HLE sometimes works with police officers on cases involving multiple arrests.

HLE handles more than 4,000 cases a year. Of course, some are simply false reports. A large percentage of cases are closed after it has been determined that no violations of the law have been committed. Sadly, many of the cases investigated do involve animals in need of some kind of relief, although not all of the owners are intentionally abusive.

My friends who pointed out that I would see terrible things if I took this job were right. But during my years at "the A" (as we referred to it), I also saw examples of incredible love and devotion between people and animals. Some of the things I saw made me laugh, others made me angry or incredibly sad. Most days, though, I went home satisfied that I had done the best I could to carry on Henry Bergh's mission. I like to think I'm the kind of person Bergh would have wanted to work there.

The stories in this book are based on actual cases I handled while working for the A. In each of them, I was amazed by the people and the animals I encountered. I hope they touch you as deeply as they touched me.

—*Tina Salaks*

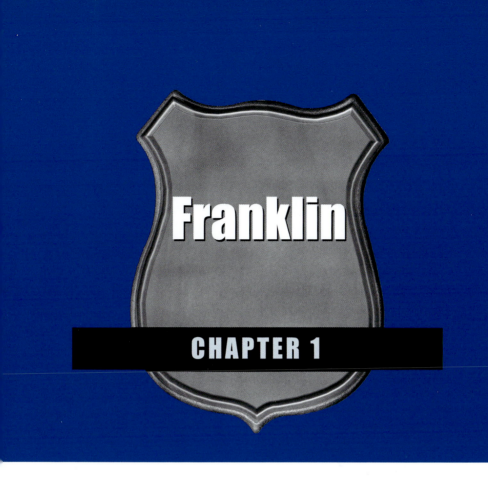

Franklin

CHAPTER 1

S ometimes I think the best cases I had were the ones that came as a complete surprise. In the summer of 2000, I was still a rookie agent when I accidentally got caught up in the most memorable chase scene of my career.

That steamy day in June, I spent the morning investigating cases in Queens and Brooklyn. When I finished up there, I headed back down the FDR Drive into Manhattan. I had just exited the drive at Ninety-sixth Street and was waiting to turn up Second Avenue toward headquarters when I heard a police car coming down the avenue, sirens wailing urgently.

It was the tail end of rush hour, and cars were still creeping along, some blocking the intersection at Ninety-sixth and Second. I turned on my rack lights to help get the cars moving so the police could get through. That's when it appeared amid the shimmering heat waves: a small, fluffy, whitish animal dodging cars as it trotted and then cantered down Second Avenue.

"Oh my God," I said out loud. "It's a lamb!"

Right behind the lamb came the police car, sirens and lights still blaring and flashing. I realized then that the cops weren't after a criminal—they were chasing the lamb.

For a minute, all I could do was stare in amazement as the lamb made his way down the avenue, weaving through the busy traffic, the police car tailing him. When the lamb reached the intersection, he swerved off Second Avenue and darted past me, headed east on Ninety-sixth Street. The police car followed, and I made a quick U-turn and joined the procession. Then the lamb hesitated; he was either tiring or it had suddenly dawned on him that he might be lost. I was relieved that he hadn't kept going—the busy FDR Drive was just fifty yards ahead. The police car stopped, and I pulled over right behind them.

The police officers and I got out of our vehicles slowly, trying not to make any noise or motion that might startle the lamb and set him off running again. I sidled over close enough to talk to the police, keeping an eye on the lamb.

"Where'd this little guy come from?" I asked the cops.

One of them, a sergeant, spoke up. "We were on a routine patrol up in Harlem when this sheep," he gave me a questioning look, to which I responded with a nod, "just ran right out in front of our car."

"That was up around 123rd Street," the officer added.

I couldn't help wincing. The poor thing had run for thirty blocks. But how did he get out on the New York City streets in the first place? Then I remembered. "There's a slaughterhouse up in that area. The lamb must have escaped from there."

The sergeant nodded in agreement. "Yeah, I bet you're right."

"Out of the frying pan into the fire," the officer joked.

I pretended to laugh. More like out of the fire into the frying pan, I thought grimly, wondering if the lamb had escaped the slaughterhouse only to become a victim of heatstroke. I ran a finger around my collar and thought wistfully of my air-conditioned patrol car. The temperature had to be in the nineties, and it was about as humid and sticky as a day in Manhattan in June could get. I've spent some time down South, and I have to say, as hot as it gets down there, I think it's even worse here. Somehow, all the pavement intensifies the heat. I glanced at the lamb, which stood panting near the curb about fifty feet from us. He looked pretty bedraggled, but he still kept a wary eye on us.

One of the cops waved an old, dried-up piece of clothesline he had scrounged from somewhere. "We can use this to catch him."

"I think we can do better than that." I opened the trunk of my car and pulled out the dogcatching equipment: two cotton rope lassoes, plus a pole lasso, with the loop at one end and the rope run through the pole to give you more control over an animal. I hesitated for a moment, then decided to bring it along, just in case. It was probably overkill, but I'd never handled a frightened lamb and had no idea how strong he'd be. "Might need this, too," I muttered, pulling out a net.

I couldn't help wincing. The poor thing had run for thirty blocks. But how did he get out on the New York City streets? Then I remembered. "There's a slaughterhouse up in that area. The lamb must have escaped from there."

I handed out my equipment to the cops, who looked doubtfully at it, then at me. I could see I was going to have to be director of operations here, although I was sure no expert on sheep. "You go around that way." I gestured to the sergeant. "And we'll come from this side."

The officer and I started slowly toward the lamb, panting by the side of the road. His eyes showed white around them from fright, and he was trembling and skittish and so filthy he was more gray than white. The poor thing was breathing so hard from his long run in the heat that I thought he might have a heart attack. Plus, he was sporting enough wool for several two-ply sweaters. I don't eat much meat anyway, but I vowed at that moment to never eat lamb again; in fact, the terrified look on the poor animal's face made me think seriously about becoming a strict vegetarian right then and there.

The sergeant began to ease around the young lamb, giving him plenty of room so he wouldn't feel crowded. But before the sergeant could cut off the escape route, the officer next to me made a sudden move and spooked the lamb. The lamb wheeled and darted past the sergeant, who lunged and made a swipe with the lasso but missed. The frightened lamb bolted down Ninety-sixth Street and then, to my horror, ran right up the exit ramp, straight onto the busy FDR Drive.

"Oh, no," I said and sprinted after the lamb, with the two cops right behind me.

All I could think was, this was going to be a disaster. The lamb would get hit by a car, or cause an accident, or both. I hoofed it up the ramp, praying that we could nab him before the worst happened.

Miraculously, the little troublemaker had run right across the southbound lanes without getting hit. Then he hopped over the median and turned south—straight into the oncoming northbound traffic. The cops and I didn't hesitate for a second. The three of us plowed across the three southbound lanes, dodging cars, and began to give chase, also running head on into traffic.

You know that little voice inside that we all have, the one that wakes up in situations like this and warns us if something we are about to do is really, really stupid? Well, mine was yelling at me to stop and get off the darn highway before I got myself killed! I kept running anyway. I think the panicked look on the lamb's face would have haunted me forever if I had given up.

Three or four blocks down the highway, the lamb seemed to be pulling even farther ahead, and I felt my heart sink. How he could find the strength to run faster after all this I couldn't imagine, but he was definitely getting away. Cursing my stiff uniform boots, I kept pounding along, hoping the lamb would tire before I did.

As we passed Gracie Mansion, home of the mayor, I heard the sergeant gasping into his radio. "Request direct with 19th Precinct. . . . Can you stop traffic on the FDR northbound? Be advised, am in pursuit of a lamb running down the drive."

I somehow found the breath to chuckle when I heard 19th Precinct's puzzled response. "10-4, Sergeant. . . . Did you say *lamb?*"

"That's a copy," the sergeant panted.

The three of us continued hoofing down the drive. Some of the drivers saw us chasing the lamb and would shout out directions when he unexpectedly changed lanes. Unbelievably, even more drivers were asking us, "What are you chasing?" They had seen the animal but actually didn't know it was a lamb. City slickers!

By now it seemed as if we had been running forever—sort of like those bad dreams you have where you're trying and trying to run, but your legs move in slow motion. The lamb, however, showed no signs of slowing. I kept expecting at any moment to hear the dreaded sound of screeching tires, followed by a thud, but thankfully that didn't happen. Saint Francis, the patron saint of animals, must have been working overtime that morning.

By the time we hit Eightieth Street, the three of us were ready to collapse, but I could see we had finally started to gain on the lamb. The highway department had stopped traffic ahead of us, and one driver had the presence of mind to turn his car at an angle, blocking the lamb's escape route. As we got closer to him we slowed, afraid of spooking him again, but the lamb was finally too tired to run anymore. We managed to get a rope around him, and the poor little guy just gave up and lay down, completely exhausted. The chase was over. Red faced and dripping with sweat, the three of us just stood there for a moment, too winded to speak. Talk about hot pursuit!

"So what do we do with him?" the sergeant asked uneasily when we had caught our breath. Both cops were looking at our woolly prisoner as if he were some kind of freaky alien from *Men in Black*. I realized that, while these guys probably had plenty of experience with dangerous criminals, they had no idea how to handle a little lamb.

"Cuff him and write him up," I deadpanned, holding out my handcuffs.

The officer laughed. The sergeant didn't seem to appreciate my little joke. Neither one of them made a move toward the lamb. I guessed it was up to me to decide what to do next.

I stepped forward. "He won't bite," I said, and carefully scooped him up off the hot asphalt.

The lamb was heavier than I had expected, and still breathing way too fast. NYPD had managed to get one of its sector cars to the site; I slid into the backseat and held the lamb on my lap. His eyes were wide with terror, and I could feel his heart pounding so fast and hard it scared me. I was pretty sure he was going into shock. The ASPCA has an excellent medical center: Bergh Memorial Animal Hospital. I asked the cop to get us there as fast as possible. It wasn't far, but the poor little guy was in such distress, I was afraid he wouldn't make it.

We had radioed ahead to tell the doctors we were coming, but the look on their faces when I walked in carrying a lamb was priceless. They could hardly believe it. I filled them in on the details of what had happened as they started to treat him. The little guy was severely dehydrated, and his heart rate was through the roof. For a while, it looked as though he might not make it; but as he cooled off and the fluids kicked in, his vitals started to come back to normal, and it seemed he would be OK after all.

The vet filling out the lamb's chart glanced up at me. "We have to call him something. Got any ideas?"

I thought about our heated chase down the FDR and it came to me instantly. "Franklin," I said with a grin.

Then I smelled something and realized it was me—little lambs are really cute, but they sure do stink!

Later that day, when I had cleaned up and finished my case reports, I went to check on Franklin. He seemed to be recovering nicely and was quietly munching some hay. "Boy, are you lucky," I told him. "If you weren't such an escape artist, you'd be a lamb chop by now."

When I got back to my office, the Public Relations Department had left messages for me. "The *Daily News* wants an interview," they told me. "So do channels 2 and 4." Word about Franklin's mad dash for freedom had gotten out, and every major newspaper in the city was running an article on it. Some even put it on the front page. The story also ran all day on several different TV and radio stations.

Franklin stayed at Bergh Memorial for several days and made a complete recovery. He now has a home at the Green Chimneys farm and animal sanctuary in upstate New York. He's apparently quite a celebrity up there, and people still ask about the "lamb on the lam."

Sadie

CHAPTER 2

Every once in a while, I wish I could just wave a magic wand and make everything better—make a sick animal healthy, make an old one young again. And if I had only one wave, I would have used it on Sadie.

The summer I met Sadie and her owner was an unusually hot one. But aside from the large number of calls about animals in distress because of the heat—dogs left in cars, kittens or other animals in the sun in a pet shop's window, carriage horses showing signs of respiratory distress—we kept getting calls about a woman trying to walk an apparently injured dog along the Grand Concourse in the Bronx. The problem was, we couldn't seem to get enough specific information from the reports to locate the animal. Even the callers we spoke to directly couldn't identify a cross street where the pair had been sighted or give an address for the woman. Whenever I was in the area, I kept an eye out for the woman and her dog, but I never spotted them.

Finally, one day luck was on our side. A caller made the same report about a woman walking an injured dog. The caller had been driving by, saw the dog and her owner, and realized something was wrong with the animal. She hung around long enough to see which building the woman went into and gave us the address. She didn't know the apartment number, but I was sure I could find them.

"I hope you get the person," she said. "It was horrible, the way that poor dog was hobbling along."

"We'll do everything we can, ma'am," I assured the woman. I promised myself I'd do whatever it took to locate the suffering dog. It amazes me how many people won't seek medical treatment for their supposedly beloved pets.

The address was in an area full of huge prewar buildings that had at one time been elegant but were now dingy and decrepit. I entered the once grand lobby, saddened by the state of neglect, and looked around for the floor directory in hopes of finding the super; he'd surely know the woman I was looking for. Before I had crossed the lobby floor, however, I saw a frail elderly woman coming down the stairs. She was slowly leading an aged and limping dog. *That's got to be her*, I thought.

"Hello," I said to her, making sure to sound friendly.

"Hello," she replied, keeping one eye on the dog, who was painfully negotiating the last couple of steps.

"Hi, puppy," I said to the dog. She was a collie mix, mostly brown, with white points. She was too sick—or too hurt—to wag her tail. She looked at me for a moment, her brown eyes dulled with pain, then sat down panting, clearly grateful for the rest. "What's your dog's name?" I asked.

"Sadie," the woman said.

"Sadie's not feeling too well, is she?" I asked gently. The woman didn't reply, so I went on. "I'm Officer Salaks. I'm here to check out a report of a sick dog."

The woman looked surprised. "Are the police looking for me? I didn't know they investigated animals."

"I'm not with the police, ma'am. I'm with the ASPCA. We've been getting calls about your dog." I gestured to Sadie. I was trying not to sound accusatory, but I really hate to see an animal suffering from neglect. Clearly, Sadie needed treatment by a veterinarian and could probably benefit from painkillers. It bugs me how people will pop an aspirin whenever they need it but never think about giving a pet something for pain.

At that moment, Sadie slowly and shakily stood up and looked at her owner. "It's time for Sadie's afternoon walk," the woman told me firmly.

"Do you mind if I walk with you?" I asked hopefully. Some people are suspicious and resistant to anything outside their normal routine. I figured a walk with Sadie's owner would give me time to persuade her to get some care for Sadie, although the more I looked at the dog, the more I began to think she was probably beyond help.

Clearly, Sadie needed treatment by a veterinarian and could probably benefit from painkillers. It bugs me how people will pop an aspirin whenever they need it but never think about giving a pet something for pain.

Besides whatever else was ailing her, the poor dog had a tumor on her right shoulder the size of a softball. And she was ancient. The hair around her eyes and muzzle was nearly all white, with those two dark brown eyes peering dully out at the world she had no doubt once enjoyed. I wondered if she could see or even hear. She had the rough, shaggy look of a very old animal that no longer sheds out its heavy winter coat, and she was panting heavily from the heat of the day and her struggle to walk—and I use the term loosely. She could hardly move the front leg with the tumor, and arthritis had taken its toll on the joints of her hind legs. Once again I had to wonder, *how do people let their animals get to this state?*

By the time she made it to the curb, Sadie was exhausted. But she seemed content to sit and rest while I talked with her owner, whose name was Mrs. Hart. I pulled out my memo book and began to jot down some information. I was still hoping I could talk Mrs. Hart into having Sadie treated by a veterinarian. As I scribbled notes, I tried to think of the best way to bring up the subject. I hoped I could talk the woman into taking Sadie to a veterinarian.

"Boy, Sadie's really having a hard time getting around, isn't she?" I began. "And it looks like she has a tumor on her shoulder there," I added. "Have you taken her to a veterinarian recently?"

Mrs. Hart peered at me intently. "Oh, yes," she said. "I took her right away, when the lump first began to show. That was about a year ago," she reflected.

"And what did the vet say?" I asked, expecting to hear the usual story about how an expensive operation was necessary, and she couldn't afford to pay for it. *So the poor animal pays the price*, I thought bitterly.

"We saw two different doctors, and they both told me the same thing. They said the only way to remove a tumor like that was to cut off her leg. I was hoping that if they did surgery they'd be able to save her, but they told me it was no use; they didn't believe it would stop Sadie's cancer," Mrs. Hart told me.

"Oh," I said, somewhat mollified. "What did they do for her?"

"They said the only thing they could do was to give her some medicine for her pain."

I began to feel a bit guilty. Here I was all ready to give this woman a lecture about basic humane care, and it seemed as if she'd already done more than most people would.

"Why don't you come up with me?" she added. "I can show you the receipts from her medicine."

Something told me I didn't need the proof, but I decided to go anyway. "All right," I agreed.

"Come on, Sadie," Mrs. Hart chirped.

Sadie looked in Mrs. Hart's direction, panting slowly, but didn't get up.

"Come on, Sadie," Mrs. Hart repeated, a little louder and more cheerily. "It's time to go home." But poor old Sadie was spent. Mrs. Hart gave the leash a light tug, and Sadie let out a quiet little yelp.

Mrs. Hart sighed. "It's gotten so hard for her," she said sadly. "Just wait a minute. My brother is coming, and he will help me to get Sadie up the stairs." She was looking up the street anxiously.

"How long does it usually take you to get down to the street with Sadie?" I asked.

"Oh, about twenty minutes, I guess . . . sometimes longer," she admitted. "It would be so much easier for her if we had an elevator."

"What floor do you live on?"

"The fourth floor," she replied stoically, and my heart went out to this elderly pair.

While we waited for her brother, Mrs. Hart began to reminisce fondly about Sadie's younger days. When the brother showed up, he appeared to be older than Mrs. Hart, and she had to be in her eighties. I couldn't imagine how either one of them was going to carry a sixty-pound dog up three long flights of stairs.

"I'll take her up for you," I offered. Gingerly, I got my arms around Sadie and hoisted her as gently as possible to my chest. She struggled for a moment, letting out another yelp, but then gave up and decided to tolerate my holding her. I followed Mrs.

Hart and her brother through the shabby lobby and started up the stairs with Sadie in my arms.

How on earth this poor old woman managed to get Sadie up and down these stairs every day was beyond my comprehension. I couldn't imagine her elderly brother carrying the dog back up for her every time they went out. Nor could I imagine Sadie walking up all these stairs by herself in the state she was in. I wondered, *how long had they been going on like this?*

You see all kinds of terrible things as an HLE special agent. After a while, some part of you hardens to it. You have to, or you'll never make it in this job. And believe me, by that time I had seen plenty. An old dog with cancer should have been no big deal, right? But as I started up the second flight of stairs, my throat began to ache, and my eyes filled with tears. By the time we reached the fourth floor, I was biting my lip to keep from crying, grateful that I was still wearing my sunglasses. *Get a hold of yourself,* I told myself fiercely, while Mrs. Hart unlocked the door. *What kind of an example are you setting for law enforcement?*

Sadie began to struggle. I set her down and quickly swiped at my eyes under my shades, hoping no one had noticed my momentary lapse. Mrs. Hart opened the door and we were greeted by the happy little growls of a younger dog, some kind of shepherd mix. Sadie crept inside and settled herself in the living room on a worn rug.

Mrs. Hart showed me her carefully organized receipts. She had spent over $2,000 on vet bills for Sadie, plus the cab fare getting her into the city to the veterinarian's office. One glance around the apartment at the shabby old furniture told me that Mrs. Hart wasn't exactly well-to-do.

"I can see you've done your best to get care for Sadie," I said, embarrassed that I had ever thought her neglectful. The old dog was lying quietly while the shepherd mix romped happily around her.

"I have always loved dogs," she replied. She paused, then added, "Come in here, and I'll show you my children."

I followed her into the dining room, where she gestured to an old china cabinet. Glass-paned doors enclosed the top shelves, and stuck all around the edges of the panes were dozens of photographs. Mrs. Hart's "children" were all the dogs she had owned since the 1930s. They were all different breeds. Some were dressed up for the photographs or for holidays in little party hats or outfits, and they were all adorable. As I looked at the photos, I realized that I was standing next to one of the kindest and most loving pet owners I would probably ever meet, which made it even harder for me to say what I knew I had to say.

"It doesn't seem that Sadie's medication is working anymore, does it?" I said to Mrs. Hart. "She seems to be in a lot of pain."

Mrs. Hart sighed. "I know," she admitted. "I know she doesn't have much longer. She's been such a good girl. I hate to see her like this." She paused. We were still looking at the photographs of the other dogs, but I knew we were both picturing Sadie. "Such a wonderful dog . . ." she murmured. Then her tone changed. "But she's not always this bad," she said brightly. "You know, I think the heat makes it harder for her. She has better days."

As I looked at the photos, I realized that I was standing next to one of the kindest and most loving pet owners I would probably ever meet, which made it even harder for me to say what I knew I had to say.

Now it was my turn to sigh. Sadie's life was nearly over. She was suffering; there was no telling how much pain she was in, and she was maxed out on her meds. It was time to say good-bye. But how could I tell this woman she needed to have one of her "children" put down?

I decided to propose a transition. Putting down a beloved pet is a hard decision for anyone; I thought if I get could get Sadie out of the house, it might help Mrs. Hart distance herself enough to see that it was time to let Sadie go.

"Bring Sadie in to the ASPCA animal hospital," I suggested. "The doctors there might have another opinion. At least they might be able to give Sadie something else for her pain."

"Oh, I don't know about that," Mrs. Hart said.

"And if they can't help her," I said gently, "they can put her to sleep. The doctors there are very good."

I did my best to persuade Mrs. Hart to bring Sadie in, but she started to get flustered, so I let it go. I guess she knew it would be the last time she saw her dog, and she just wasn't ready to make that decision.

"Take a little time to think about it," I said. "Here's my number at work if you have any questions, or if I can help you in any way." I hated having to leave them like that, but there was nothing else I could do. The dog was under a vet's care for her tumor—if she wasn't, I could have impounded her; but even if that had been the case, I still would have tried to get the owner to bring her in. If I took the dog, it would have just been more trauma for both of them. Before I left, I gave Sadie a gentle pat. "You're a good girl, Sadie," I whispered. Then my eyes started to sting again, and I quickly made my exit.

That was my last day of work for the week, but even after I had wrapped up my cases for the day and gone home, I couldn't stop thinking about Sadie. My first day back at work the following week, I went straight to my boss and told him about Mrs. Hart and Sadie.

"It's not a cruelty case," I explained. "But they need help. I don't think this woman will bring the dog in on her own, but I think she'll come with me if I go pick her up."

This is not something we ordinarily do, but after he heard the case, my boss agreed. "Go get them," he told me. "And drive her home afterward," he added. I left his office smiling.

But when I went to check my voice mail, I had a message from Mrs. Hart. The message didn't give any specific details, so I called her back.

The phone rang several times. I waited anxiously, picturing Mrs. Hart laboring up all those stairs with Sadie. I was just about to hang up when Mrs. Hart answered the phone.

"This is Officer Salaks, with the ASPCA," I said when I heard her voice. "How are you doing? How's Sadie?" I asked.

"Well, I just wanted you to know that the night after you came, Sadie died in her sleep," Mrs. Hart said.

I felt a surge of relief for poor old Sadie and a flood of sadness for Mrs. Hart. I know she must have been aching with grief, but she kept her voice steady as she went on to say that she appreciated my concern for Sadie and herself. She was having Sadie cremated and wanted to invite me to the pet cemetery for a little memorial service.

I wanted to attend, but the ceremony was in the middle of a busy work day for me, and I couldn't slip away. Mrs. Hart sent me a lovely thank you card with a touching note, thanking me for my kindness to her and Sadie. For a long time I kept it taped to the inside of my locker. I still have the card tucked away in a drawer. And I still have Sadie in my heart.

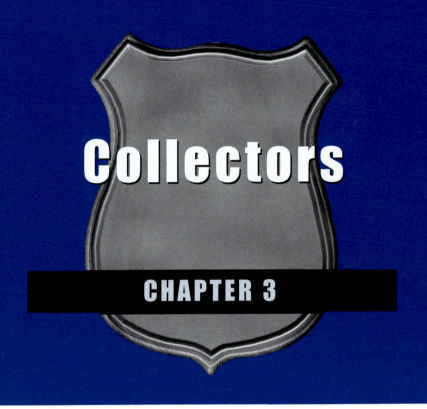

Collectors

CHAPTER 3

S ome people collect cars. Other people collect those little china figurines. A friend of mine collects old dishes, and I collect small pieces of antique silver. Even some animals have been known to stash piles of stuff in their holes, or their nests. We all like to accumulate things: I guess it's left over from the days when we depended on our ability to gather to survive. But I will never understand what makes people want to collect animals.

You never forget your first experience with a collector (also known as a hoarder) case. I know mine is forever engraved in my memory—and my nostrils. I was still a rookie agent when I got a call to check out the care and condition of some cats at an address on Flatbush Avenue in Brooklyn. It was an apartment directly over a furniture store. I parked my car, crossed the street, and before I had even stepped up on the sidewalk, the store owner came hurrying out to talk to me.

"I hope you're here to do something about that nut upstairs," he said with a wave toward the building behind him and a look of total disgust.

"I'm here to check out some cats. Are you the owner of the building?"

"Nah, this is my store. But that crazy cat lady, she's ruining my business. You can smell them all the time—it's terrible. People walk into my store, they get a whiff, they turn right around and leave. It stinks." He sounded pretty pissed.

"That bad, huh?" I said politely.

"The entryway stinks too," he added, motioning to the small door that led to the upstairs apartments. "And it attracts flies. I hope you're gonna do something about her."

I was trying to listen patiently, although what I really needed was to get upstairs and talk to the owner of the cats. But later, after my first encounter with "that crazy cat lady," I understood what he was so upset about. Visiting a collector is bad enough—living or even working all day next to one would be a nightmare.

I did catch a whiff of "eau de feline" when I entered the building. By the time I got to the second floor, the whiff of cat had become more an actual stink of cat urine. I followed my nose down the hall and found the apartment. An open garbage bag filled with empty cat food cans sat outside the door, adding to the smell. Plenty of flies were buzzing around it, but what really got my attention were the roaches crawling all over it.

I hate cockroaches.

With a shiver of disgust, I stepped gingerly around the bag and knocked on the door.

"Who is it?" a woman's voice asked.

I gave her my name and told her I was from the ASPCA. "I need to check on your cats. Can I come in?"

I thought she might say no, in which case I might have to try to get a search warrant. In retrospect, I wish she *had* said no, but after a moment I heard the familiar clicking of locks turning and chains sliding, and she opened the door.

Nothing could ever really prepare you for your first encounter with a collector. I guess that's why it was never mentioned in my training. That moment is permanently etched in my mind—and I really wish it weren't. I don't know what shocked me more: the smell of cat urine that was so strong I almost gagged, the forty or so cats running in every direction, or the hundreds of roaches crawling around my feet.

Stay cool, I told myself. *They're not going to attack.* But right then I would have sold my soul for a giant hazmat suit. In fact, if I'd had a choice between stepping into that room full of bugs and facing a bunch of gangstas up in the projects, I'd have chosen the bad guys, no contest. At least I might've been able to talk some sense into them. (Did I mention that I *hate* cockroaches?)

It's still just about one of the hardest things I've ever had to do—really—but I managed to step inside that apartment. It was a small studio, and I was standing in the tiny kitchen area. I imme-

You never forget your first collector case. I know mine is forever engraved in my memory—and my nostrils.

diately had the feeling that bugs were crawling on me. *Just take a deep breath* I thought, then *BAD IDEA! VERY BAD IDEA!* as I did my best not to toss my breakfast right there. I had a better idea: *maybe I should just* hold *my breath*. I got my stomach under control and tried to breathe through my mouth as much as possible.

"How bady cats do you have here?" I asked, sounding as if I had a bad cold.

"You know, I'm not really sure. They love to hide."

"I see," I said, edging away from a really big roach crawling up the wall near me and trying to avoid a suspicious-looking smear on the floor. As I moved through the kitchen, I noticed the oven door standing open. Suddenly, two cats popped out of it and went tearing by me as if they were on fire. Shocked, I looked at the woman.

"Oh, don't worry," she said. "The oven hasn't worked in years. The cats just like to hide in there."

"I guess you must order a lot of takeout," I said, looking for any excuse to lighten things up.

She either didn't get it or she didn't hear me. The woman—I'll call her Peggy—was older and fit the typical profile of the animal collector. Collectors are generally white women in their sixties or seventies, although some collector cases are men. They're usually retired or unemployed, living beyond their means to feed their collection. They seem to genuinely care for their animals but can't comprehend that the conditions they're forcing the animals to live in are unhealthy and improper—never mind that the Health Department doesn't allow humans to live in those conditions. Some of them suffer from psychological disorders such as obsessive-compulsive disorder as well. I know of collectors who hoard so much junk there's barely room for their animals. One guy had so many magazines and newspapers piled up in his house that I had to follow him down a narrow pathway through them to get to the bedroom where his animals were. Another lady in a house in Queens had been visited at one time or another by just about every agent at the ASPCA. They never knew exactly how many cats she had, since she would never let anyone inside her house, but they were all healthy—she'd open the door a crack and show the agents each animal one by one! The good news about collectors is, although they're quirky, they're usually quite kind, and I've never known them to be dangerous or threatening in any way.

I wish I could say the same for insects.

Slowly, I worked up the nerve to venture past the kitchen into the living room–bedroom area. Stray cat litter crunched under my feet, and fluffy wads of dusty cat hair floated up, then settled again as I passed. Every step I took seemed to freak out the cats. They ran away from me, hissing, and scrambled for cover, startling other cats—who came running out, saw me, and started the cycle all over again. I'm sure most of them had never been socialized, and the ones that hadn't been born in this hell-hole had certainly forgotten what the outside world was like.

There wasn't much furniture: a chair taken over by cats, so shredded and covered with fur I couldn't really identify the color or the fabric it was made of, and a bed (a term I use loosely). The animals had torn holes in the bed and had burrowed their way in. When I came close to it, cats started jumping out of the mattress and even the box spring. I couldn't see how there was room for a person to actually lie down and sleep there—if anyone could sleep knowing all those roaches were crawling around everywhere. *How on earth does she live like this?* I wondered.

The freak show wasn't over yet. When Peggy showed me the bathroom, I couldn't believe it. More cats were living in the bathtub, sink, and toilet, all of which had stopped working. I had this vision of cats clogging the pipes all the way down to the basement. I didn't have the nerve to ask how she managed without a working toilet. To tell you the truth, I didn't want to know.

I slowly began to acclimate to the horror around me. (I had to stop breathing through my mouth for fear of inhaling too much cat hair, and while I can't say the smell wasn't horrible, at least I had stopped gagging.) Peggy of course didn't seem to mind the wretched conditions. Granted, she was used to it, but how on earth could anyone think this was normal?

I asked her to show me the litter boxes; I had counted only three during the tour, and it turned out that's all there were. With that many cats, she should have had fifteen or twenty. She had both dry and canned cat food on the premises and three or four aluminum turkey roasting pans she was using to feed the cats. There was water available—I guess the kitchen sink was still cat free. As I wrapped up my little tour of the apartment, one of the cats jumped up on the back of the hairy chair and gave my shoulder a friendly rub. I scratched his chin, and he purred happily. Then another one hopped up on the arm and begged for some attention. So at least a couple of them were friendly. I petted them both and tried to think of a way to convince Peggy that this was no way to keep animals.

What I really wanted to say was, "How can you live like this?! Don't you know this is totally gross? It's disgusting even for animals to have to live like this, never mind humans. You say you love your cats, but if you really did, you wouldn't force them to live in this . . . this . . . cat sty!"

In a corner, I spied a mother cat nursing six teeny kittens. They didn't look healthy. In fact, they all seemed to have a nasty upper respiratory infection. "Have you taken any of your cats to a veterinarian?" I asked her.

"No . . . no, I haven't."

"I see." I sighed.

"Are you going to arrest me?" she asked.

"No, no," I reassured her. "You're not breaking any laws, unless your lease says 'no pets,' but that's none of my business."

Peggy became quite chatty once she realized I wasn't going to give her a hard time. The cats had adequate food, water, and shelter. New York State law doesn't regulate the number of animals you can keep in your house. Peggy went on to tell me that she was on Medicare and that most of her Social Security check went to feed the cats.

Her story was typical of many collectors: She had started with three cats. Her intentions were good. They were strays, dirty and skinny, so she rescued them. Of course, she never got around to spaying or neutering them, so a few months later, the female had kittens. Peggy knew she ought to find homes for them, but they were so cute, and the mother cat was so attached, she just couldn't give them away—and after all, what's five more? So then there were eight, and then several months later another litter, and so it goes. The problem with collectors is they just can't say no to another animal; they take in every stray that needs a home, and pretty soon it's out of control. Collectors are blinded by love, and their judgment is impaired along with the size of their wallets. (So far, I've never met a rich collector.)

"I love them. I just try to help them. People know I love the cats, so they find a stray and bring it to me. How can I say no?" Peggy asked me.

I said what I would find myself saying to all collectors I met. "I know you love them, but it's better to take excellent care of three or four cats instead of keeping so many in such poor conditions."

Unfortunately, my little speech would usually go in one ear and out the other. Collectors are convinced that they are right and that they are somehow saving all their animals from a terrible fate. The next step with a collector like Peggy was to try to get her to surrender some or most of her animals. This would require some careful planning.

When I first walked into that apartment and saw all those cats living like that, I thought, *Oh my god, I've got to get them out of here.* But as I started counting, I realized that our adoption center probably wasn't going to be able to handle forty or so cats all

"I love them. I just try to help them. People know I love the cats, so they find a stray and bring it to me. How can I say no?" Peggy asked me.

at once. And, as I soon learned, as bizarre as it seemed to me, Peggy really did love her cats. She wanted to keep them. Getting her to surrender any of them was probably going to take some real convincing.

"Peggy, I think you're in over your head here, don't you?" She didn't say anything, so I went on. "Would you let me take some of your cats? We'll find them a good home, and then you won't have so many to worry about."

"Oh, no, I could never get rid of them. I love my cats."

Every once in a while, you come across someone who's secretly relieved to give up their animals. You make them feel good about it, tell them they're doing the right thing, that the animals will be better off, yadda yadda yadda, and they give up without much of a fuss. Not Peggy. I was using my best persuasive tactics, but she was having none of it.

I looked around at all those cats and decided I had to at least make a dent in the number. "How about this?" I tried. "Let me just take that mother cat and her kittens. They're sick, you know. I can get our vets to treat them, and they'll be just fine. Just think of all the happiness they'll bring to some family."

"The kittens . . . ," she said doubtfully.

"I tell you what. You think about it. I'm just going to call my boss and let him know that your cats are doing all right. I'll be back in few minutes, OK?"

"OK," she said.

I tiptoed through the buggy kitchen and beelined it out of the building. I've never been so glad to be out on the street breathing the "fresh" city air. The exhaust fumes from a passing bus seemed like perfume.

I knew there was no way I could get Peggy to give up all her cats, but I was hoping to get her to at least surrender the mother and kittens. Then we'd see what could be done about the rest. First, I called our adoptions center to make sure they had room. They did, so then I called my boss to let him know what was going on. We had a discussion about Peggy's age, income, and living conditions, and we agreed that there wasn't any reason to charge her with cruelty. We seldom arrest collectors, partly because they tend to be little old ladies, and partly because intent is an issue: they do intend to take care of their animals, and usually the only thing they're withholding from them is a clean apartment.

Speaking of which, Peggy's apartment was a disaster. This was definitely a case in which the Department of Health needed to step in. I called them right away and explained the situation. Sometimes they don't have the authority to get involved, but if Peggy met the qualifications, the Department of Health would get someone over there to clean things up, and Adult

Protective Services could provide whatever other aid Peggy might need.

Going back up to Peggy's apartment wasn't quite as shocking as my first trip there, but it sure wasn't much better.

"Peggy, we have room for the cat and the kittens at our Adoption Center. How about I take them for you and get that respiratory infection treated before it gets any worse?"

She was still very hesitant, but I wasn't giving up. "Look at those beautiful kittens. Think of all the joy they will bring to someone's life. And you have so many already. It's not fair to keep all that joy to yourself, is it?"

"But what if they don't get adopted right away? You won't put them to sleep will you?"

I reassured her that we wouldn't euthanize the cats, and she finally agreed to let me take them. I loaded the mother and her babies into a cage with a soft towel in the bottom and said good-bye to Peggy and her collection. When I got into my car and closed the door, I was horrified by how bad I smelled. I was happy that I'd managed to rescue at least a few of the cats, but I was dying to get into a hot shower and out of my stinking clothes before I crawled out of my skin!

The next week, I went back to check on Peggy's cats and to see if I could get her to let me take a few more of them. She asked about the mother and babies, and I told her they'd been treated at our hospital and were all doing fine. I told her I was sure we'd have no trouble getting the kittens adopted as soon as they were old enough. We chatted for a few more minutes, and she eventually agreed to give up some older kittens. After I dropped them off, I called the ASPCA's mobile Care-A-Van and asked if they would talk to Peggy about spaying and neutering the remaining thirty or so cats.

That was my last visit with my first collector. Since Peggy wasn't being charged with cruelty, the case was officially closed. I heard that the Department of Health did get involved in this case, so I guess they got things cleaned up. We never got another complaint about "that crazy cat lady," which is fine with me—I get the shivers just thinking about it.

I learned a lot about being a better agent from this case. First, it was a good example of how you have to pick your battles. If I had charged into her apartment and started lecturing her about the conditions, she probably wouldn't have given up the few cats she did. I guess you can catch more cats with milk than you can with vinegar—and you can catch more bugs with cats than you can with honey! Second, it was a good reminder that you can't always go in and try to be an animal rescue superhero; sometimes your job is just to leave the animals better off than they were before you came on the case. And the last and most important lesson? Always have a good insecticide spray in your squad car in case you have to visit a collector—ick, ick, ick!

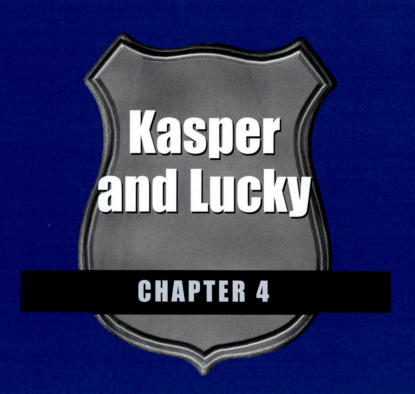

Kasper and Lucky

CHAPTER 4

I cruised over the Verrazano-Narrows Bridge toward Staten Island, enjoying the view. It was a clear, sunny day in late winter, and the light glinted on the bright blue water far below. A sailboat skimmed along, and if you didn't look at the bare branches on the opposite shore, you could almost believe it was summer. Anyway, spring was right around the corner, and boy was I glad. Being from Wisconsin, I don't really mind the cold, but like everybody else I was looking forward to longer days and ditching my winter coat. And thanks to the milder weather, it had been a calm week at the A.

Typically, we'd get a lull in the number of complaints this time of year and another in the fall. I think everybody in HLE was grateful for the lighter workload, although we knew it wouldn't last. On this sunny Saturday, most people were at home enjoying the start of the weekend. For me, it was the last day of my work week, and for a change I had only one new case to check out: an anonymous call saying someone had moved out and left two dogs behind.

I found the address quickly and pulled up in front of the house. There were no cars in the driveway or parked out front, but there were still curtains in the windows. I could hear dogs barking somewhere behind the house and wondered if the noise had been the real reason behind the call.

Barking dog complaints are supposed to be handled by the Department of Environmental Protection. When the department gets a noise complaint, it sends out a form letter to the owner of the dog. If the barking problem continues, it may send someone out with a decibel meter to measure how loud and frequent the barking is. Then the department may issue a summons. But the whole process takes such a long time that, when they discover that their first call goes nowhere, people often call the ASPCA. Typically, it goes like this:

Caller: Yeah, I want to report a dog. It's barking all day, and the owner's never there. Can you come out and do something about it?

ASPCA Dispatcher: Ma'am, you need to call the Department of Environmental Protection. The ASPCA does not investigate reports of barking dogs.

Caller: Well, what do you do?

Dispatcher: We investigate reports of cruelty, and in all the cases we investigate, we ensure that the animals have adequate food, water, shelter, and medical attention when necessary.

Caller: Well, this dog is really thin. I don't think they're feeding him. You should send someone out to check on him.

Dispatcher [with an inward sigh]: What is the address?

Most of these cases turn out to be nothing more than disgruntled neighbors and unhappy dogs. Dogs hate to be alone, so when their owners go off and leave them all day, they bark. It's separation anxiety. If they have a companion, such as another dog, or if the owner is around most of the time, it usually doesn't happen. I wish more dog owners would pay attention to the emotional needs of their pets. It would save animal cruelty investigators a lot of useless trips.

I knocked on the front door and waited. The barking got louder, but no one answered the door. I could see through the partially open curtains that there was still furniture in the house, which indicated that someone might still be living there. *They're probably just away for a few days,* I thought. We sometimes got complaints like that, in which the owners left the dogs in the yard while they went on vacation and had a friend come over to feed and water them. With nobody around for days, the dogs bark like crazy and annoy the heck out of the neighbors, but it's not a cruelty case. I posted a Notice to Comply on the door, giving the owner twenty-four hours to contact me, and went around to the side of the house to check out the source of the barking.

There was a four-foot cyclone fence enclosing the side yard and part of the backyard. As I approached, a beautiful German

Dogs hate to be alone, so when their owners go off and leave them all day, they bark. It's separation anxiety. If they have a companion, such as another dog, or if the owner is around most of the time, it usually doesn't happen.

Shepherd Dog—a big male—ran up to the gate and stood with his paws hanging over the top. He was barking, but he was also wagging his tail a mile a minute. He appeared to be healthy, not malnourished or very dirty, which are two conditions you usually see in abandoned animals. He seemed friendly and happy to get some attention, but I approached warily. *He could jump that fence in a second,* I thought, while I offered him the back of my hand to sniff.

He sniffed at my winter coat and stopped barking, enthralled with the scent. It may sound crazy, but smelling like a dog can actually be a good thing. An animal might be very uptight, but as soon as I got near, they'd catch a whiff of all the creatures I'd been around that week and forget about everything but the smell. It worked like a charm. I've lost track of how many times people told me their dog wasn't good with strangers, only to have the animal sniff once and latch on to me like Mary's little lamb.

This dog seemed friendly even without being hypnotized by my smell, so I went ahead and opened the gate. Once inside the yard, I stood still and let him sniff me all over while I patted him. "Good boy," I told him. I was impressed at what a lovely dog he was. I couldn't see anything obviously wrong with him.

The other dog was still barking frantically but didn't come to the gate. I figured he must be tied up, so I walked around to the backyard to check on him. The German Shepherd followed me, still sniffing happily at my legs.

Behind the house I saw the second dog, chained to a picnic table. He was still barking excitedly and trying to run and jump, but the chain had become hopelessly tangled around one of the picnic benches, so he only had about three feet to move. This dog had some German Shepherd in him, too, but mixed with something else, so he wasn't as handsome as his friend. Still, he was cute: rowdy and puppyish, even though he was almost grown. I approached him slowly and let him smell me as well. He stopped barking and didn't growl, just kept wagging his tail. I quit worrying about either of the dogs being aggressive and went over to the picnic bench to see if I could get him untangled. While I worked on the chain, I took a good look around the yard. I didn't see any shelter or dishes for food and water, but that didn't mean anything was wrong. Some owners bring their pets inside the house to feed them or when the weather is bad. I decided I'd give the boys a little snack for their good behavior and wait to hear from the owner.

When I came back from the van with the open can of dog food, both dogs were doing the happy dance. "Here you go, guys," I said. I dumped out some food for each and watched as they dove toward it and began to chow down rapidly. That was when I noticed something abnormal-looking on the back of the younger dog's neck.

I put a hand on him carefully; some dogs are very possessive about their food, but he hardly noticed. Then I was able to examine his neck more closely. I knelt and gently parted the fur. Where the chain collar slipped through the ring, the repeated rubbing and pulling had cut into the dog's neck. It was ugly and matted with old blood, skin, and hair. I felt my stomach lurch at the sight of it.

How could they let this happen? I was as angry as I was disgusted. You would see a wound like that only after days or weeks of repeated irritation. This poor dog's neck was so mangled that parts of the chain were embedded deep in the wound, even though the rest of the chain hung slack under his throat. I wanted to take it off right then, but I didn't dare; it was surely going to hurt. The vets at the ASPCA would have to remove it.

He was licking up the last greasy crumbs of dog food. "Hey, fella," I said, scratching his ears gently. "There's more where that came from. How about you come with me, and I'll get that old chain off your neck?"

For once, I was glad to be driving the van. It was a big old clunker, cumbersome in traffic and not the most comfortable thing to be driving around the boroughs all day, but it had two large animal cages in the back. I would be taking the healthy dog as well as the injured one into protective custody, so the cages would come in handy. It's a good idea to have another agent along to help when you're taking multiple animals, but at the time no other agent was even remotely close.

"Hey, fella," I said, scratching his ears gently. "There's more where that came from. How about you come with me, and I'll get that old chain off your neck?"

I decided to take the bigger dog first, since he seemed to have some manners. I slipped a rope around his neck, and he came right along with me. In fact, he was so cooperative that if loading him were an Olympic event, his scores would have been 9.5, 9.6, 9.2 (the Russian judge), 9.7, and so on! I couldn't believe how easily he jumped up into the van and walked inside the crate just like it was home.

The second dog was another story. When I got him loose from the picnic table, he was so happy to be free that he was jumping around like a kangaroo. I was trying to coax him along with me without putting any pressure on his wound, but he wasn't leash trained (or any kind of trained, apparently) and had no clue what I wanted him to do. Getting him from the yard, around the house, and out to the van was an exercise in creativity, to say the least. When I got him to the van, he seemed eager to join his friend, but how to actually get inside the van was a complete mystery to him. He did eventually figure it out, half jumping and half with an assist by me, and from there it wasn't too hard to get him into the crate. Thank goodness for friendly dogs.

I called Base to let them know I was bringing in two dogs and to have them alert the hospital that one was going to need treatment immediately. Then I headed back across the bridge toward Manhattan.

Both dogs tolerated the long ride pretty well. At the ASPCA hospital, the healthy dog was taken to the holding area, and I went with the injured dog to the examining room. Two of us lifted him onto the table without much trouble, and then the veterinarian started to examine the neck wound.

Collar injuries are very common. People put a collar on a dog when he's young, then they forget about it, or they are too lazy to buy a bigger one. The dog grows; the collar doesn't. Slowly, it cuts into the animal's neck, causing abrasions and all kinds of trauma to the neck area. In this case, the collar wasn't too small; there was some excess length hanging at his throat. Apparently, the chain collar had started rubbing his neck, and with so little room to move, the constant pressure from the weight of the picnic bench had caused the chain to cut deeper and deeper into the raw skin. A long section of the collar was now thoroughly embedded in the wound. *This poor dog*, I thought. I could not imagine how painful it must have been. And worse, this was not a sudden injury. It had happened slowly over a long period of time. The veterinarian showed me how in some places the dog's skin had actually grown over the chain.

"He's going to need surgery to remove this," the vet told me.

I shook my head sadly. I decided that I was going to do everything in my power to find out who was responsible for treating the dog this way.

While technicians prepped the dog for surgery, I went up to my office to write up the case. Then I got the camera and went down to surgery. I never liked going into surgery; I'm not great with blood. But this case would have to be documented, so I took a deep breath and told myself, *This is no time to be queasy.*

I tried to stay detached as I watched the vet tech shave the anaesthetized dog's neck. I snapped several photos of the area. It was bizarre seeing the metal chain apparently growing out of the dog's neck. I kept shooting while the veterinarian carefully cut through the tender skin and tediously extracted each link of the chain. It took quite a while, but she did a spectacular job. Finally, she handed me the chain, bloody and encrusted with bits of old skin and hair. I snapped a few more pictures as she began stitching up the long jagged wound. "Great job," I told her, then headed upstairs to log the evidence.

That night, I had a hard time falling asleep. I was so disgusted with the owner of that poor young dog. *Be glad you found them when you did,* I told myself. It was some comfort to know that at least now the dogs were in good hands. That night, they would be warm and comfortable for a change.

The next week, when I went back to work, the first thing I did was check my voice mail. The owner of the dogs hadn't called—not that that was a big surprise. Then I checked to see if the owner's phone was still on; it had been disconnected. When I went back to the house, I found the Notice to Comply still taped to the door. The search for the owner wasn't going to be easy, but I had just begun. I was taping another Notice to Comply over the first when I lucked out—I spotted the mail carrier making his rounds.

I introduced myself and explained that I was following up on a cruelty investigation. "Any idea where these people moved to?" I asked him.

"Coney Island," he told me. "They left a forwarding address."

More good luck. A quick trip to the post office, and I would at least have an address.

While I was talking to the mail carrier, a curious neighbor peered out from the front door of a house across the street. A minute later, she approached us.

"You from the ASPCA?" she asked.

"Yes ma'am. I'm looking for the owner of a couple of dogs we found in the backyard of this house. Do you know anything about them?"

"Oh, sure. You know, they just went off and left those dogs. Moved away and left 'em all alone back there. They were barking all the time. They're nice dogs, but they bark. I felt sorry for 'em—no food, no place to get outta the cold. I was throwing food to 'em, over the fence. A coupla other people did, too."

That explained why the dogs weren't emaciated. I was writing down the information as fast as I could. "Do you have any idea when they moved out?"

"I don't know, about a month ago, maybe longer."

So if it hadn't been for the neighbors throwing food to them, the dogs would have starved.

She went on. "That one that was chained, I felt so sorry for him, but I didn't dare go in there. I told my son; he was gonna try to get the chain untangled so the poor dog could move. I kept thinking maybe they would come back for 'em, but they never did. Poor dogs," she shook her head and tsk-tsked.

I got on the radio and asked Lisa, the agent who covers Brooklyn, to meet me out there. Armed with the forwarding address from the post office, we drove out to Coney Island and tracked down the apartment building.

You'd think that the people who abuse animals would look the part. Sometimes they did, but more often they just looked like regular people. When we knocked, a petite Filipino woman in her early thirties answered the door, holding a very small baby over her shoulder. Not exactly the type you'd expect to be arresting on animal cruelty charges. I began to have my doubts.

Lynn Pacas was suspicious of me at first but did eventually give what seemed to be a reasonable explanation of how the dogs, whose names she said were Kasper and Lucky, had been left at the house alone. According to her, she and her boyfriend had acquired the dogs several months before. Kasper, the big German Shepherd Dog, had failed the police K9 program and was given to them by a police officer friend. Lucky was adopted from a local shelter. The baby came along, and then things didn't work out between Lynn and the boyfriend. He left, so Lynn moved in with her mother.

"He told me he was going to take the dogs," Lynn said. "I never went back there. I got kids to take care of."

As if on cue, the infant woke up and began to fuss.

"I know you're busy," I said. "I appreciate your taking the time to talk to me. Could you give me your ex-boyfriend's name and address? We'd like to talk to him about the dogs."

"I don't know where he lives now," she said, sounding miffed. "I don't see him. I don't talk to him. He don't even give me any money for the baby."

You'd think that the people who abuse animals would look the part. Sometimes they did, but more often they just looked like regular people . . . . Not the type you'd expect to be arresting on animal cruelty charges.

"Can you tell me where he works?" I asked hopefully.

A few days later, I caught up with Lynn's ex-boyfriend. I'd called him at the auto supply store where he worked, and he had agreed to talk to me. Lynn had told me a couple of things about him that convinced me that this time I was going to be meeting up with a real tough-guy animal abuser, so I put on my best tough-girl officer face and knocked on his door.

Rick Malinosky was a big guy, into cars, tae kwon do, and tattoos. He had been living at his parents' home in Queens ever since he and Lynn had split up several months before. I was surprised to find him friendly and genuinely interested in answering my questions.

"I guess you're here about the dogs, huh? Are they OK?" he asked anxiously. "She told me she was gonna take care of 'em. I hope nothin' happened to 'em."

When I told him that I had taken the dogs into custody because they were abandoned and that Lucky was hurt, he was really upset. He told me how bad he felt that he couldn't take the dogs when he left, but there was no place to keep them at his parents' house.

"I love dogs," he said, sounding passionate. Then he showed me a tattoo of one of his dogs on his upper arm, so I knew he wasn't lying. You don't go out and get a tattoo of something you don't care anything about. He signed over the dogs to me reluctantly, seeming genuinely pained that he couldn't take them. I promised to keep him posted on Lucky's condition.

"I'm so sorry," he kept saying. "Believe me, if I could keep 'em, I would. Hey, you're not gonna put 'em to sleep are you?" he asked me.

"Absolutely not," I reassured him. "We'll keep them in custody until they're adopted."

Once again, what I expected and what turned out to be the reality were two completely different things. Lynn Pacas had a criminal record longer than a giraffe's neck. A little sniffing around at the precinct turned up a few outstanding warrants for her arrest. A little more investigative work, and I learned that Pacas was the owner of the house where Kasper and Lucky had been left. So far it was a case of "he said, she said," but after hearing both sides of the story, I thought that the "he said" seemed a lot more believable than the "she said." In the end though, it all boiled down to who was responsible for the care and custody of the animals. Pacas was the owner of the property, so the responsibility for Kasper and Lucky—and for Lucky's injury—was hers.

New York state law says: "Any person who owns or has custody or control of a dog that is left outdoors shall provide it with shelter appropriate to its breed, physical condition and the climate." Kasper and Lucky were left in the yard with nothing but a picnic table. The law also specifies that the person who has custody of the animal is responsible for any medical treatment the animal may need. Not only was Lucky in need of medical treatment, his injuries were a direct result of being abandoned by his owner. I went over all the evidence with our attorney, and got the OK to arrest Pacas on animal cruelty charges. But before I went out there, I put in a phone call, just to make sure she was at home.

A woman with a Filipino accent answered the phone.

"Hi, this is Special Agent Salaks, from the ASPCA," I said. "Is Lynn Pacas there?"

"No. Lynn is not here. She moved out."

"Who is this?" I asked.

"This is her mother."

"She moved? Where did she move to?" I asked casually, not buying it for a minute. Lots of times people will lie when they feel threatened, but if you're patient, they eventually cave in and tell the truth.

"She moved to the Philippines," the mother announced.

"The Philippines? That's pretty far away. You know, I was just there the other day talking to her. She told me she moved in with you so you could help out with the kids, right?" I listened hard, hoping to hear kids in the background. "She didn't say anything to me about moving. When's she coming back?"

"I don't know. I have to go. Lynn is not here," she repeated firmly.

"Well, if you see her, tell her to give me a call at the ASPCA, OK? I need her to sign some papers about her dogs."

The law specifies that the person who has custody of the animal is responsible for any medical treatment the animal may need.

I hung up the phone, disappointed. She had evaded me this time, but I wasn't ready to give up yet. I wasn't buying the moving story. Nobody with outstanding warrants just ups and moves out of the country. Plus, she had a couple of kids. I was sure she was just hiding out. The question was, where? I decided to pay a little visit to the super of the building.

Back at the Coney Island address, I went into the lobby and struck up a chat with the doorman, asking him if he knew where I might find Lynn Pacas. Then I found the super and quizzed him about her whereabouts. They both said they'd seen her two days ago. And neither she nor anyone else in the family had said anything about her leaving the country. I left my card with them, and they agreed to call me immediately if they saw her. I went back the next day and sat on the building for a while, hoping I'd spot her trying to slip back in.

Unfortunately, Lynn Pacas turned out to be the one who got away. She was still in New York after all—just not where I thought she'd be. I ran her Social Security number and checked with NYPD. Turns out they had picked her up on one of her open warrants the day before I got there. She was already in the Bedford Women's Correctional Facility, a women's prison upstate.

If HLE had arrested her first, we'd have notified NYPD, so they could add their charges to the arrest. However, because we were charging her with a misdemeanor and not a felony, the assistant district attorney did not want to do a "takeout order," removing her from prison for one day to process our charges and add them to her record.

Pacas was already in prison, and the dogs were no longer in her custody. Under the circumstances, would adding the misdemeanor charge have mattered? It probably would have added some time to her sentence. Did she deserve it?

Sometimes when we make an arrest, I do end up feeling sorry for the perpetrator. People do things out of carelessness or ignorance that end up hurting animals even though the people didn't directly abuse them or intend them harm. And Pacas did have little kids. But whenever I became frustrated with this case, I'd think of that bloody chain embedded in Lucky's neck. I'm still sorry we didn't get her. That was the only animal cruelty case I ever had where the owner was never charged.

With Pacas in jail, the case was technically closed, but I've never been able to forget an animal that I've taken into custody, and Kasper and Lucky were no exceptions. I dropped by Adoptions to see them whenever I had a chance. Lucky's ugly neck wound was healing well, and Kasper always greeted me with lots of happy tail wagging. I was still impressed with how gorgeous and well-trained he was and mentioned it to one of my fellow agents who was friends with a cop up in Rockland County. When the officer heard about Kasper, he came down to see him, and I think you could call it love at first sight. The officer adopted him, and Kasper, the failed K9, went to a happy home upstate.

One down, one to go. But getting someone to take Lucky was going to be a challenge. His neck had healed nicely, and he was a good-looking dog, but he was young and hyper and had little obedience training. People adopting a grown dog expect that he'll at least be housebroken. Nobody wanted to take on a project like Lucky. The weeks turned into months, and he was still languishing in Adoptions.

The concern in cases like this is that a dog can go "kennel crazy." Although the ASPCA has volunteers and staff who walk the dogs, play with them, and work on their obedience training, some dogs just can't take the confinement of a kennel. These dogs become aggressive and sometimes have to be euthanized; though rare and very unfortunate, it does happen. After four months, I was worried about Lucky. I kept mentioning him to friends, hoping someone would be interested in adopting him. Poor Lucky. He'd already lived in two homes and ended up in animal shelters. If any dog deserved a break, he did.

Finally, one of our volunteers took pity on him and took him into foster care. Friends of hers eventually adopted him. I heard that he was a big handful at first, once escaping the new owners' yard by jumping the eight-foot fence surrounding it. I told her to tell the owners that Lucky might have a future as one of those Frisbee dogs. He was certainly athletic enough. Fortunately, the people who took him in had plenty of patience, and I hear that Lucky's now settled down and doing fine in his third home. I guess it's true: the third time's the charm.

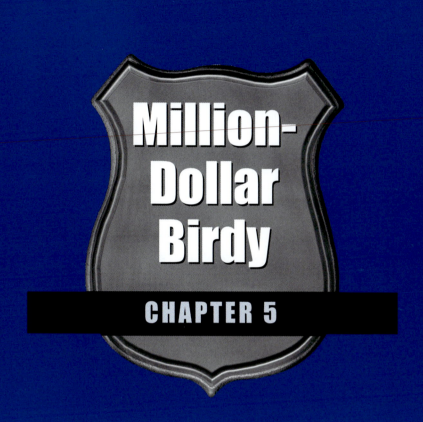

Million-Dollar Birdy

CHAPTER 5

M aybe it's a nondescript warehouse in the Bronx, with peeling paint over old brick and rusty metal gates sprayed with graffiti covering the exits. It could be a dim basement apartment in Brooklyn, with half a dozen families living in the space, or a pet shop in Queens, with a room in the back that you can't see from inside the shop. Or it might be a rambling, rundown movie theater with the name *Social Club* on the marquee. All of these different spaces in very different areas of the city have something in common: in certain seasons of the year, often on weekends, and usually late at night, they may become arenas where dog- or cockfights are held.

Dog- and cockfighting are illegal in the United States. In New York State, the law says that anyone who engages in the practice of fighting animals; who owns or trains animals for fighting; who breeds, sells, or offers for sale any such animals; or who owns the premises where any of these acts occur is guilty of a Class E felony, punishable by a fine of up to $25,000 and up to four years in prison. The law also says that anyone who owns, possesses, or keeps an animal under circumstances that suggest an intention to fight the animal is guilty of a Class A misdemeanor, punishable by a fine of up to $15,000 and up to a year in prison. If you're a spectator who pays admission to an animal fight, or if you make a wager at such an event, you're also guilty of a Class A misdemeanor. If you are arrested on any of these charges, you can also be charged with causing or permitting animal suffering, which can add an additional $1,000 fine to your sentence, along with another year of jail time.

Nevertheless, the fights go on.

The history of animal fighting goes back thousands of years. The first laws prohibiting animal fighting were established in the 1800s. Today, animal fighting is just as established and traditional as the laws forbidding it; in the cultures in which it's most common, the methods of keeping and training animals for fighting, the rituals surrounding the fights, and the history of the champion bloodlines of the animals are still handed down from one generation to the next. Because it's illegal, information about where and when fights are being held or animals bred or trained is closely guarded within the cultures

The law also says that anyone who owns, possesses, or keeps an animal under circumstances that suggest an intention to fight the animal is guilty of a Class A misdemeanor, punishable by a fine of up to $15,000 and up to a year in prison.

in which it occurs. The only way to investigate animal-fighting rings is for law enforcement agents to try to go in undercover and get evidence that animals are being used for fighting. To do that, you have to be able to penetrate a very protected underground subculture. For an investigating agent, that means if you're a male and black or Hispanic, you might have a chance at infiltrating a dog- or cockfighting ring by buying paraphernalia associated with fighting or by making it into an event as a spectator, where you could then initiate a raid. If you're a white girl from Wisconsin? No way.

Still, the ability to sniff out the animal criminals seems to be in my genes. A routine complaint about a woman with too many cats turned out to be my link to uncovering a small cockfighting ring.

At the address, a run-down building in the Bronx, an elderly woman I'll call Martha answered the door. I thought I was going to have another collector on my hands and was already mentally preparing for the worst: the smell, the hair, the bugs. . . .

"Hi, I'm Special Agent Salaks." I gave my usual spiel and asked to see her animals. As it turned out, she did have a lot of cats, but it wasn't as smelly as I expected, and the good news was that they were all healthy, with adequate food, water, and litter boxes—and best of all, not a bug in sight! She was actually running a mini rescue operation out of her apartment, fostering homeless or abandoned cats.

I wrote down what information I needed, wished her luck, and was about to leave when she asked me, "What if I hear about cockfighting?"

"Well, if you hear of something like that going on, you could always give me a call." To tell you the truth, I was skeptical. The likelihood of an elderly white woman like Martha having any reliable information about cockfighting was pretty small. I gave her my contact information and left, not really expecting to hear from her again.

I was wrong. Less than a week later, I had a message from Martha saying she knew of a place in the same neighborhood where roosters were being kept and fought. I still had my doubts. We'd get reports like this sometimes when it was just a pet rooster somebody was keeping in a yard. That's not legal, but it's also not a fighting ring. It was a Sunday morning when I heard Martha's message, so even if it turned out to be a fighting location, the fights would be over by now and all evidence of the night's activities hidden away. I didn't want to go off on a wild chicken chase, so I decided to just make a quick check of the location before I started a major investigation.

The good thing about working Sunday mornings is that there's almost no traffic. I sailed up to the Bronx in record time, hitting all the green lights. I found the address: Martha had described a building with a basement where the activities were supposedly going on. When I checked the basement door, I found it secured with a heavy-duty chain and padlock. From somewhere beyond the door, I could hear roosters crowing. I couldn't see into the courtyard from the front of the building, but maybe I could view it from upstairs, so I decided to try my luck.

I climbed a flight of stairs to the second floor and knocked. I said to the tenant, "I'm looking for a dog that's supposed to be in the courtyard. The basement door is locked. Could I look out your window and see if there's a dog back there?"

The woman let me in and showed me to a window overlooking the yard. Martha was right. There were some cages back there with what appeared to be roosters in them, at least one shaved for fighting. I took a good look, mentally recording the details. Then I told the tenant, "I don't see a dog. Maybe it's the wrong address. Sorry to bother you." I thanked her and made my exit.

I reported my findings to my supervisor. A few days later, a team of agents broke into the basement and seized about eight roosters in the "cock hotel." Their chests and legs were shaved to keep them from overheating during a fight. Their combs and wattles had been "surgically" removed—often done with an X-Acto knife. There was plenty of paraphernalia used in training fighting birds, such as bottles of injectable vitamin K (given to promote blood clotting), antibiotics, growth hormones, stimulants, and steroids. There were "boxing gloves"—small rubber domes that are strapped over the roosters' spurs to minimize injury when they are sparring in training for fights. In an actual fight, the spurs are often covered with longer, sharper artificial spikes called gaffs, which can puncture lungs and eyes. The birds often break each other's bones with their strong beaks. The fight isn't over until one bird is too injured to fight anymore. The odd thing is, although it's clearly cruelty, the men who own and train these fighting birds, the *galleteros*, seem to genuinely love their birds. They tend to be older Hispanic men, usually Dominican or Puerto Rican. (One guy who was eventually busted for running a breeding operation was so involved in the business that he was known as the Don of Cockfighting.) These guys actually tear up and beg agents not to take their "babies" if they are present when birds are seized.

So if they love their birds so much, why fight them?

Money. On one raid I assisted with, we confiscated $17,000 in cash and nearly twenty gamecocks. For the men who run the rings and for the breeders (champions birds may be worth up to $1,000 apiece), cockfighting is an extremely profitable, cash-only sideline business. Animal fighting usually goes hand in hand—or paw in claw—with gambling. Drugs and prostitution are also associated with the fights. Tens, even hundreds, of thousands of dollars may change hands at a cockfight, between admission charges, liquor sales (without a license), and wagers on the fights. The owners get a big percentage of the take. It's easy to see why they cry when they lose their birds—they're losing a lot of liquid income.

While cockfights tend to be well-planned and organized events run by older men, dogfights are different. The owners

The odd thing is, although it's clearly cruelty, the men who own and train these fighting birds, the galleteros, *seem to genuinely love their birds.*

tend to be younger, often black and Hispanic men in their teens or twenties. The dogs are usually pit bulls, or American Staffordshire Terriers, trained to fight from puppyhood. Their tails and ears are usually docked—through at-home surgeries performed with knives or scissors. Although some fights are organized, more are spontaneous, especially in urban areas. They take place at random locations: abandoned buildings, parks, basketball courts. The same illegal activities surround the fights—drugs, gambling, and so on—and just as it does with cockfighting, thousands of dollars change hands. But unlike cockfighting, dogfighting in New York and in other major cities where it's prevalent is usually an extension of gang violence.

Because dogfighting is less organized and therefore harder to infiltrate than cockfighting, often the only way the ASPCA investigates dogfighting is when they get a report of injured or dead dogs at a location. Winning dogs live to heal their wounds and fight again. Dogs that lose are often left injured, dying, or dead in the building or area where the fight took place. Other signs of dogfighting are chains or ropes from which bait is hung, used to train the dogs to take hold of another animal and to strengthen their jaws; metal or wooden sticks used to break the hold of an animal that won't let go; and conditioning equipment such as treadmills. Sometimes there will be a pit: a square enclosure of some kind where the dogs are fought. Vitamins, hormones, stimulants, and steroids are also used on fighting dogs.

When the ASPCA finds injured fighting dogs, the animals are taken to the hospital for treatment. Some of them recover, only to hang around in Adoptions for long periods of time. Some of the dogs can be rehabilitated and adopted, but others, the ones too badly injured or too aggressive ever to become pets, have to be humanely euthanized.

Seized gamecocks have no future. They're so "juiced up" on steroids that they can't be kept with other birds—they would kill them. Gamecocks are always euthanized.

Pitting animals against each other is a barbaric sport that causes pain and suffering to the animals. If you know of it, or see evidence of it, please report what you know to your local law enforcement agency, to the SPCA in your area, or to the ASPCA.

There's nothing entertaining about animal fighting. But in a high-tension situation, sometimes the best thing you can do is keep your sense of humor. At one cockfighting raid, I was stationed outside the building, assigned with some NYPD officers and a supervisor to guard a locked exit. Other officers and agents had already entered the building and were in the process of rounding up participants and spectators and making arrests. We were monitoring their progress on our radios.

A few minutes went by. Then we heard what sounded like a stampede coming down the stairs on the other side of the exit door. People started yelling and banging on the door, but it wouldn't open from their side. These guys were desperate to get out of there; the banging and yelling got louder and louder. The police officers and I exchanged looks, and I know we were all envisioning the same thing: all these people running from the police and the ASPCA, thinking they would escape through this door, only to find that it was locked from the outside and they'd have to go back and give up. Finally, one of the police officers yelled through the door, "It's no use. You're stuck. Turn around." Eventually, the banging subsided as they went looking for another way out or surrendered.

It was pretty funny, although we were trying not to laugh. We would have felt like idiots if the door had given way.

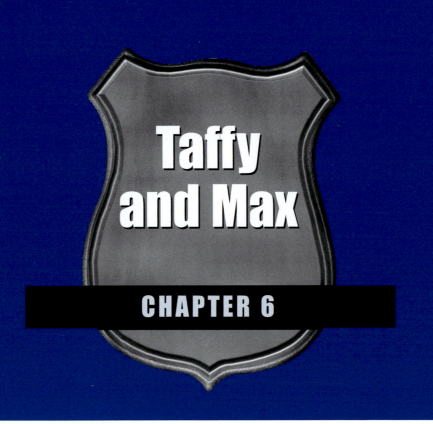

Taffy and Max

CHAPTER 6

Winter 2003 was one of the worst winters most New Yorkers had seen in a while. It snowed every week in January, and we had so many days of brutally cold weather, it felt like I was back in Wisconsin. The weatherman said it was the coldest winter in about ten years. I guess the only creatures who didn't mind the frigid temperatures were the polar bears at the Central Park Zoo.

Naturally, Humane Law Enforcement was very busy. We received dozens of calls each day, mostly reporting dogs left outside without proper shelter. Sadly, some animals froze to death before we could get to them. Needless to say, we took these reports very seriously, so when I got a call to check on two dogs at a Vernon Avenue address in Brooklyn, I wasted no time getting out there.

When I'd checked the weather report that morning, the prediction was for yet another snowstorm. It was supposed to hit that night and was expected to dump a half a foot of snow on the city. I rushed through my cases, trying to cram in as many as possible, knowing I might not be able to get out the next day. Driving over the Brooklyn Bridge, I had a good view of the sky; steely gray clouds were creeping in from the northeast, just as the weather forecaster had predicted. I glanced worriedly at my watch and then pushed the accelerator a couple of miles an hour faster.

The address was a run-of-the-mill brick house in a region of Brooklyn known simply as East New York. The area is in the Seventy-fifth Police Precinct, one of the busiest precincts in New York. The yard was fenced, and I heard two dogs barking as I approached the gate. *This must be the place,* I thought. A rusty, beat-up old boat of a car sat in the driveway, and behind it I saw a large male Rottweiler chained to the wall. The good news was that he did have a shelter: an igloo doghouse, which is one of the better ones. The bad news was that he was fairly skinny. From where I stood, I gave him a quick once-over. He didn't seem to have much of a winter coat. I looked around for the second dog and saw a buff-colored Cocker Spaniel chained up a little farther down the driveway. I couldn't make out the condition of the Cocker Spaniel from there, but I could see it also had an igloo.

When I knocked on the front door, a woman answered. I guessed her to be in her sixties, an attractive Jamaican woman. She invited me in, and I began to question her about the dogs.

"Those are my husband's dogs," she told me. "I don't have anything to do with those dogs."

I was taking notes, as usual. "Have they ever been taken to a veterinarian?"

"I really don't know." She also didn't remember their names or how old they were.

"The Rottweiler looks like he's very thin. Does he have any medical problems that would explain why he's so skinny?" I asked the woman.

"You must talk to my husband about that. I don't bother with those dogs. Like I told you, I don't like dogs."

"Well, I'd like to speak with him. Would you mind giving him a call for me?"

She tried calling her husband then but couldn't reach him. I told her I'd like to get a closer look at the dogs, so she put on her coat and walked outside with me. The Rottie didn't seem to be old, but he was definitely underweight. I asked the woman to get him some food. She claimed she didn't know where the dog food was.

I've met plenty of people like her. She wasn't lying; she just really couldn't care less about animals. Still, it was hard for me not to sound irritated.

"Would you try to find him something to eat, please? Anything at all: some table scraps, some bread?"

She went in the house and came out with some bread, which she threw to the dog. He devoured it in about two sec-

A warning growl from the Rottie stopped me. Obviously, he wasn't going to let me come any closer. Luckily, the camera had a zoom lens. I stayed where I was and focused on the other dog. That's when I noticed that something was terribly wrong with the Cocker Spaniel's eye.

onds and looked expectantly at us, obviously hungry for more. I didn't have any food in the car with me that day. I was hoping the woman would feel sorry for him and go look for the dog food, but she just stood there holding her coat closed, waiting for me to get on with it. I took some photos of the Rottweiler, then tried to ease around him to check out the condition of the Cocker Spaniel.

A warning growl from the Rottie stopped me. Obviously, he wasn't going to let me come any closer. Luckily, the camera had a zoom lens. I stayed where I was and focused on the other dog. That's when I noticed that something was terribly wrong with the Cocker Spaniel's eye.

I didn't even bother asking if the woman knew about the eye. I wanted to take the dogs right then and there, as both of them were in need of medical attention, but I had to follow the proper procedure. Since the owner of the dogs was known, I could do nothing until I actually spoke with him. He may have taken the dogs to a vet already. Given the Rottie's emaciated condition, I thought it was highly unlikely, but I had to give him the benefit of the doubt.

"Please ask your husband to call me as soon as possible," I told the woman. I left her with a Notice to Comply, stating that the dogs must be seen by a veterinarian immediately, and went back to my car. I still had a couple of cases to investigate before the end of my shift. As I headed back across the bridge, I saw the first flurries of snow landing on my windshield.

The snowstorm hit us as promised, and by morning there were several inches on the ground. The snowplows had been busy all night, so the buses were running on schedule, and I made it in to work with no problem. Unfortunately, although the snowplows clear the streets pretty well for the traffic that's already on the road, they pile the plowed snow on top of the vehicles parked along the sides of the streets; it takes some real digging to get them out. And the streets are still plenty slippery. Only two of our seven vehicles had four-wheel drive, limiting the number of cases we could see on a day like this.

I was at my desk doing some paperwork when a call came in for me. It was the owner of the two dogs in Brooklyn. I quickly pulled out my notes from the day before and began to question him.

The dogs' names were Taffy and Max. According to Raymond, the owner, a neighbor had given him Taffy, the Cocker Spaniel, about a year ago. Max, the Rottweiler, was a stray. Raymond had owned Max for about five months.

"Max is very thin, Raymond," I said. "What have you been feeding him?"

"I feed him dog food. Sometimes when I run out, I give him table scraps. He's got a lot of energy, that's why he's so thin," Raymond explained.

He's not burning up much energy chained in the driveway all day, I thought. "What's the matter with the other dog's eye?" I asked Raymond.

"Oh, Taffy, she had that eye when they gave her to me. She's all right. She's not hurting any."

"Well, maybe it hurts her and maybe it doesn't, but that eye looks serious to me, Raymond. Have you ever taken your dogs to see a vet?"

"No, I haven't."

"Well, you need to take both those dogs to the vet right away. This morning," I told him. "Taffy needs that eye looked at immediately, and Max needs to get checked out, too. He could have heartworms or some other condition that's making him stay so thin."

"This morning? Just you look at the snow. How you expect me to get out in that? Listen to me. I told you: Taffy had that eye when I took her. There is nothing wrong with my dogs," he insisted.

"Now you listen, Raymond. I am telling you, you need to take those dogs to the vet."

"I'm telling you, my dogs don't need to go to no vet."

I didn't really think he'd volunteer to take them that morning; after all, the roads weren't in great shape. The local veterinarian might not even be open. What I was looking for was

One thing we try to do when assessing a cruelty case is determine whether the animal's owner means well and has just let things slide, or whether there's willful negligence. I was looking for a good faith effort, but this guy wasn't trying even a little bit.

some indication that he was willing to get the dogs seen by a vet. One thing we try to do when assessing a cruelty case is determine whether the animal's owner means well and has just let things slide, or whether there's willful negligence. I was looking for a good faith effort, but this guy wasn't trying even a little bit.

Raymond promised to call back later, but from the tone of his voice I was pretty sure he was blowing me off. We all know there are times when you should trust your intuition, and I felt that this was one of those times. I had a bad feeling about this guy Raymond, and I decided I wasn't going to wait around until he called back (if he called back). I ran the case by my boss, and we agreed that I should go get the dogs. I quickly rounded up what I thought I would need, including cages, a noose, a net, and some food, went out to load up the car, and—

"Oh, man!" I said with a groan. The car was buried under a mountain of plowed snow. All I could see was the roof and part of the windows sticking out. I needed to get to Brooklyn fast, but first I would have to dig the car out.

Usually, we would go out alone during the day, but in snowy weather or when going to pick up multiple animals we would partner up. I went back for the snow shovels and my partner, Michelle, and together we started digging. Having grown up in Wisconsin, I was used to shoveling snow, but I guess my technique was a little rusty. Even with Michelle helping, it took half an hour to get down to the wheels. We were both exhausted by the time we finished, but there was no time to stop and rest. We loaded up the car as fast as we could and headed for Brooklyn.

I was anxious to get to those dogs. The more I thought about the Cocker's eye, the more worried I became. When we finally got to the house, I saw her, still chained up outside. I was relieved to see that at least the eye didn't look any worse. Then my heart sank.

"Oh, no," I said.

"What is it?" asked Michelle.

I pointed to the chain lying curled on the driveway. "The Rottie's gone."

Raymond's wife answered the door again. She didn't seem the least bit fazed at seeing me again. She answered my questions in the same disinterested tone she'd had before. I asked her where Max was; she didn't know. I asked where her husband was; she didn't know that either.

"Did your husband take the dog to the vet?"

"I don't know," she said, maddeningly calm.

"Thanks," I said, through clenched teeth.

The only good thing was that without Max guarding the driveway, we could finally get a good look at the Cocker Spaniel. Michelle and I walked around to the side of the house where Taffy was chained.

As we came close, the little dog started jumping and barking happily. She was obviously friendly, and she was thrilled to have some attention.

"Hey, Taffy. Hey, little girl," I said and stooped to pet her. But when I got a good look at her face, I was appalled. Her left eye was grossly deformed, swollen to nearly the size of a golf ball. It was covered with a brownish film and bulging out of the eye socket. It looked as although it was literally about to burst.

"Oh, God, look at that," my partner said.

"How do people do this?" I muttered. How do people who supposedly care for their pets just let them go on living with some awful condition that can, and obviously should, be treated? I scooped up Taffy and carried her to the car, where she curled up happily in the backseat.

As we pulled away from Raymond's house, I was feeling bad that we'd been too late to help Max. But I was glad that we'd been able to take Taffy. And she seemed just as grateful to be with us. Every time I glanced back at her, she wagged her tail at me. "I bet this is the first time she's been warm all winter," I said to Michelle.

"What do you think they did with the other dog?" she asked me.

I shook my head. "You know, that guy was so annoyed that he even had to speak to me. He didn't want anything to do with taking the dogs to the vet. I'll bet he just got rid of the Rottie. He probably would've gotten rid of this one, too." I glanced back at Taffy, who was dozing peacefully on the backseat.

"You think he just dumped him somewhere?"

"Probably," I said gloomily. I knew Michelle was thinking the same thing I was: it's easy enough to drive a dog somewhere in the city and put him out when no one is looking. I pictured Max nosing around spilled garbage in the snowy cold of a dark alley, growing thinner every day. Soon enough he would starve or be hit by a car. I sighed.

Then I had a thought: the guy obviously didn't want to go to any trouble, and the city animal shelter was less than half a mile away. I felt my intuition kicking in again. "Hey," I said, "let's check CACC."

"You think he dropped the dog at the shelter?" Michelle moved into the left lane and turned onto Linden Boulevard.

"It's so close," I said hopefully. "It's worth checking out."

Less than five minutes later, we pulled up in front of City Animal Care and Control in Brooklyn. (It is now called the NYCAC&C, but it's the same organization.) "Be right back," I told Michelle, and headed inside.

I located the manager of the animal shelter and asked her to check the records for a young Rottweiler dropped off by a man with a Vernon Avenue address. I folded my arms and leaned over the desk, trying to read the computer screen along with her as she scrolled down the records of animals brought in during the past forty-eight hours.

"I think this may be the one you're looking for," she said at last. "The address checks out. A guy came in a couple of hours

How do people do this? How can people who supposedly care for their pets just let them go on living with some awful condition that can, and obviously should, be treated?

ago with a Rottie. Pretty starved looking. He stated that he found the dog."

"He did. Only he neglected to mention that he's been the owner of the dog for the five months since he found him."

She gave me a disapproving look. "Sounds like a real nice guy." She got up and came around the desk. "You want to see the dog?"

I told her I did, and she had a staff member bring him out. When I saw him, I felt my heart give a little thump of gladness. "That's him," I said with relief, jotting down the information in my notebook.

Max was much friendlier off his chain and out of the cold. He wagged his stump of a tail and let me pet him. They gave him some food, and he scarfed down a king-size bowl of it while I took some photos of him for my records.

I had the shelter place a cruelty hold on Max so he couldn't be adopted until he had put on some weight and the case had been decided by a judge. Then Michelle and I drove back to the ASPCA with Taffy.

The vets there have a scoring system to assess the physical condition of the animals we bring in. It's called the TACC score, which stands for Tufts Animal Care and Condition score. On a scale of 1–5, Taffy was only a 3—a pretty poor score for a small dog. She had a cataract that had somehow become detached and was causing all the swelling and fluid buildup in her left eye. The vet didn't think they could save it. And her eye wasn't the only problem. She had mammary tumors all over both sides of her chest.

"She's an older dog, so she's not a great candidate for surgery," the examining vet told me. "We might just have to leave things as they are with her."

I watched her gently probing the lumps on the little dog's belly. Taffy was taking it calmly, just enjoying the attention. Something about that dog just took hold of me then. I'm not sure why, because I really tried (really!) not to get attached to the animals I worked with. But this one was different. Maybe it was because she reminded me of my Cocker Spaniel, Sunshine, the last dog I had when I was a kid. Maybe it was because she was old and deserved some happy days at the end of her life. Maybe it was because she'd been through so much and was still wagging her tail and licking the doctor's hand whenever she could reach it. I just felt from that moment on that I had a personal stake in her well-being.

"Bye, Taffy," I said, giving her a pat, for which I got an enthusiastic lick and a gigantic butt-wiggling, tail-wagging frenzy. "Be a good girl. The doctors are going to fix you up."

"Please try to help her however you can," I implored the veterinarian.

"We will," she assured me.

Not long after that, we discovered that NYCAC&C didn't have a scale to weigh the animals brought in to them, so we brought Max over to the ASPCA shelter, where we could properly document how underweight he was and then monitor his weight gain. Max had a few other health issues, but in comparison with Taffy's, his recovery would be easy. Starvation is usually not hard to fix.

Taffy had surgery on her eye. The doctors removed it and sewed up the socket. A few days later, when they felt she could handle it, they did more surgery to remove the tumors in her chest. They weren't able to get them all, but they removed as many as they could. Even though the prognosis wasn't good for her, she came through with flying colors. I went down to see her when she was still in the hospital. She looked like the bride of Frankenstein's little dog with all her stitches, but she was still happy to have some attention. A few days later, I checked on her again. This time the vet techs had her out of her cage and were playing with her. She had on a big plastic cone collar, called an Elizabethan collar, to keep her from scratching at her eye, but in spite of being blind in one eye and hampered by the collar, she was dashing happily around the room, banging the collar into everything and generally having a blast. The vet techs told me she'd become a favorite of theirs. It was great seeing a dog like Taffy make that kind of recovery. There are times when we feel that our best efforts are all for nothing, but it's moments like that one with Taffy that help balance that disappointed feeling with this truth: sometimes what we do really does make a difference.

Raymond was arrested and charged with animal cruelty. He pled not guilty, and because he had no prior record, he got away with a fine and probation. The ASPCA gives owners like Raymond a choice: they can pay the vet bill for their animals, or they can sign them over to us. Raymond did what most of them do: he gave up his dogs rather than shell out any money to keep them. That left Taffy and Max safe and sound with us but needing new homes. Weeks went by, and although Max was gaining weight, no one showed any interest in adopting either him or Taffy.

About this time, I was injured on the job when my partner and I had a scuffle with a 170-pound perp resisting arrest. We got him, but both he and my partner fell on me, and I ended up on the disabled list for two weeks with my ankle in an Aircast. When I was cleared for light duty, I came back to work in the office and learned that Taffy and Max were still with us. Whenever I got a chance, I'd take Taffy up to the office with me while I did paperwork and manned the phones. She had just had another surgery to remove more tumors, so we were both recuperating and glad to have each other's company.

Agents are not required to follow up on an animal once the case is settled, but when I had seized an animal, it didn't really feel as if my job was done until that animal had a new home. Weeks went by, my ankle got better, and I was ready to go back out on the job. It was then that I started to think hard about adopting Taffy. I missed her. We had done plenty of bonding those weeks when we were both healing and spending time in the office together. She was an older dog, covered with scars and lumps, the sewn-shut eye socket marring her adorable face.

People, especially families, looking to adopt would surely pass her up for a younger, less gruesome-looking pet. I couldn't stand the thought of her spending her life in a kennel, no matter how much the staff played with her. I made up my mind: I would adopt Taffy.

Just when I had decided to take her, however, I lost the lease on my apartment. My landlord was selling the building, and I had to move out on short notice. It's hard to have to leave your home. It's even harder find an affordable apartment on short notice. But the worst part of all this was that my new apartment had a no-pets clause in the lease. I wouldn't be able to adopt Taffy after all.

I'm one of those people who believe things sometimes happen for a reason. I thought Taffy should have ended up with me and couldn't imagine anyone else loving her more than I already loved her. Her story so far had been a story of hardship, and I wanted to change that.

Well, I didn't get to keep her, but her life did take a turn for the better. Here's how Taffy found a home: One day, a volunteer was walking Taffy in the park near Gracie Mansion, her scars hidden under an Adopt Me coat. They met a woman walking her pit bull, Joey. If there's such a thing as canine love at first sight, this was it. Joey dragged his owner over to Taffy, lay down at her side, and wouldn't leave her. It turned out that Joey's owner had adopted him and also an older Rottweiler from the ASPCA. The Rottie had died recently, and Joey had really been missing his companion. The woman was considering adopting another dog, so when Joey fell for Taffy, it was a no-brainer. A week later, Taffy went home with them.

It all goes to show you, there are still plenty of happy endings out there.

Max, too, eventually found a home. He was featured at an Adopt-a-thon in Union Square, where three different families signed up to adopt him. He went to a family in Brooklyn with one kid, and I hear he is happy and thriving.

Taffy's also doing great and couldn't have a more loving home, even with me. It all goes to show you, there are still plenty of happy endings out there.

Hammer Cat

CHAPTER 7

When you spend your days investigating reports of animal cruelty, you're bound to see some gruesome sights; it simply comes with the territory. Thankfully, many cases that seem to be serious at first turn out to be just the result of a misunderstanding, mild neglect, or a grumpy neighbor trying to stir up some trouble. But of all the cases I saw in my seven years with HLE, this one stands out in my memory as being the most violent scene I ever investigated, along with having the strangest twist to the final outcome.

It was a rainy Friday, the end of a very busy week for me, but I had pushed extra hard and managed to catch up on most of my cases. I'd been driving around Manhattan all day, but now I was almost done. Except for the hiss of tires on the wet streets and the faint hypnotic swipe of the windshield wipers clearing the mist from my windshield, everything was quiet. As the car inched forward in traffic, in my mind I inched ever closer to the weekend.

Suddenly, I was startled out of my Saturday daydream by the crackle of my radio: "Salaks, are you on the air?"

At the time, we weren't using live dispatch for most cases, so if headquarters called you on the air, it was usually something serious.

I grabbed my radio and responded, "Go ahead, Base."

Base came back on the air and asked, "What's your current location?"

"Be advised, I'm currently in Midtown," I said, my curiosity increasing.

"Can you give us a landline?"

"10-4." *Uh-oh*, I thought, *this isn't going to be good.*

I pulled the car over so I could have my hands free, called headquarters on my cell phone (my "landline"), and prepared to take notes. Dispatch answered, "ASPCA."

"This is Salaks," I said.

"We have an emergency in Chelsea," the dispatcher said. "A caller stated that a man residing in the building beat his cat with a hammer."

If you're envisioning the worst right about now, so was I. Violence against animals by men usually comes with a long history, and by the time the ASPCA arrives on the scene, plenty of damage may have already been done. I jotted down the particulars in my notebook, already mentally planning the quickest route to the address and hoping I wouldn't be too late.

A call like that starts your adrenaline pumping, and I was anxious to get to the scene; but after a couple of blocks I found myself in traffic that was nearly at a standstill—so frustrating! I clenched the steering wheel and watched tensely as the traffic light ahead changed from red to green three or four times without my getting much closer to it. The mist had changed once more into a driving rain. Rain in New York always slows things down, but this couldn't be just the weather. It wasn't quite rush hour either. I turned up my wipers and tuned the car radio to a local AM station to see if something else was going on.

"…building collapse in Midtown," I heard when I found the station. The sirens of emergency vehicles sounded through the beating of the rain, and I got another surge of adrenaline on top of the one already pumping. New York was still haunted by the trauma of 9/11; news of a building collapse instantly brought terrorism to mind. The incident was on Sixth Avenue, not far from where I was going. When I finally made it to the intersection, I started my rack lights flashing and detoured east, hoping to avoid the area where the building had collapsed. I kept the radio on while I worked my way downtown and was relieved to learn that the collapse was an accident, not an act of terrorism, and that no one had been killed. *Thank goodness*, I thought, and switched off the radio so I could focus on the job at hand.

Although the whole ride downtown seemed to take hours, in reality it was probably less than forty-five minutes from when I first got the call to when I located the building and dashed into the lobby. A man and a woman were in the lobby, apparently waiting for me. I started to identify myself, but the woman spoke first.

"Oh, I'm so glad you're here. You have to help this cat." She looked to be in her fifties, was nicely dressed, and had the intense look of a cat lover. She seemed genuinely distressed.

I glanced at the gentleman, wondering if he was the suspect or just a curiosity seeker. The woman must have noticed because she quickly interjected, "This is the super. He has keys to the apartment."

He nodded in agreement.

"OK," I said. "Where is the owner of the cat?"

"He went to the hospital," the super told me.

"He had a *scratch*," the woman said, her voice dripping with sarcasm.

"I see," I said. "Do you know which hospital?"

Neither of them did. I wondered if the guy was just trying to avoid dealing with me by going to the hospital with a scratch. I would check the area hospitals later. My first priority was to see the injured animal.

"Where is the apartment?" I asked.

"This way," the super said. I followed him to the elevator, and the three of us stepped inside. During the short ride to the fourth floor, the woman told me that the building was sort of a halfway house for psychiatric patients; she worked in the building and knew most of the tenants. The suspected cat abuser was a diagnosed schizophrenic. The woman seemed to have a pretty low opinion of the guy. I always tried to be

I wondered if the guy was just trying to avoid dealing with me by going to the hospital with a scratch. I would check the area hospitals later. My first priority was to see the injured animal.

objective about people when I was investigating a case, but it was hard to fathom how a crazy guy who beat on his cat with a hammer could be a nice person.

When the elevator doors opened, right away I noticed some splotches of blood on the hallway floor. *This is not good*, I thought. Grimly, I followed the super down the hall and stood behind him while he unlocked the apartment door.

Sometimes first impressions are the strongest. I know I will never forget the chilling sight before me when the super opened that door and stepped aside.

The room looked like a murder scene. It was a small studio apartment, and nearly every surface had been sprayed, smeared, or splattered with a shocking amount of blood. Blood covered most of the floor, some of it smeared, some of it in small pools. It was all over the walls. It was all over the sheets and pillows of the twin bed.

Oh my god, I thought. For the first time since I'd met her, the woman was silent.

Could a cat lose this much blood and still be alive? Slowly, I scanned the room, trying to see something besides blood. I stepped carefully over a puddle and peered into a corner of the room, searching for the cat. Then I spotted it—a big black tom cat covered in blood. He was still alive, but he sat frozen in an awkward, unnatural position, all four legs splayed out as if he were hanging on to the floor, apparently in shock. Not far from the cat was some sort of mallet, the wooden handle covered in bloody fingerprints. I took my camera off my belt and quickly snapped several pictures to document the crime scene. Then I turned to the super.

"Can you stay here for a minute, and keep your eye on the cat?" I kept my voice calm, though my heart was galloping.

I sprinted to the elevator and pressed the button, waited about five seconds, then gave up and ran for the stairs. That the cat was still alive seemed like a miracle. If there was any chance to save him, I knew I didn't have a minute to spare; I had to get him to the ASPCA hospital.

I hurried to the car and opened the trunk, my mind racing as I pawed through my gear. I grabbed some latex gloves, a couple of towels, a pet carrier, and a large manila envelope. Then I dashed back to the building.

Thankfully, the elevator was sitting in the lobby when I returned. I punched 4 and waited impatiently for the doors to close and the elevator to move. When I got back to the apartment, the cat hadn't moved. I pulled on the gloves and eased into the room with the towels and the carrier. I was trying not to step in the blood, but it was nearly impossible. I set the carrier down and folded one of the towels to fit in the bottom. Then slowly I approached the cat, trying not to freak him out any more than he already was. Although his eyes were open, he didn't seem to notice me. I reached toward him and, as carefully as I could, bundled the cat up in the towel and placed him in the pet carrier. He was too dazed to struggle. The hammer was evidence; I placed it in the manila envelope, picked up the carrier, and headed for the elevator, glad to be leaving the gruesome scene behind me.

"Where are you taking him?" the woman asked me.

"To Bergh Memorial," I told her. "The ASPCA animal hospital."

"What are you going to do about the owner?" she demanded.

"I'll deal with him later," I assured her. "Right now, I have to get this cat to our hospital."

It was still pouring rain and the middle of rush hour, but I turned on my lights and siren and made it to the hospital in fairly good time, avoiding the Midtown jam. I had called ahead to warn the doctors that I was bringing in a cat with blunt weapon trauma and substantial blood loss, so they were ready and waiting. Quickly, I described what I knew about the cat's condition and handed him over to the doctors, who hurried him away to determine the extent of his injuries and do what they could for him. To tell you the truth, I was a little surprised that the cat still seemed to be holding his own. I kept thinking of the hammer, and all that blood.

I had a quick conference with my boss. We discussed the case and took a good look at the mallet, which turned out to be some sort of heavy plastic rather than metal, but dangerous looking nevertheless. He secured the mallet in our safe as evidence and agreed that, given the serious nature of the complaint, I should

pursue the cat's owner immediately. It was well after the end of my shift by that time, but I was no longer tired. Psych patient or not, I wanted this guy held accountable for what he'd done to that poor cat. I jumped in the car and headed back downtown. My plan was to check the area hospitals and, if the guy wasn't there, sit at his building and wait for him to come home.

There were two hospitals near the Chelsea area where I figured the man would have gone, if he really had gone to the hospital and wasn't just hiding out: one was Bellevue, and the other was St. Vincent's. On a hunch, I tried St. Vincent's first.

When I walked into the ER, it was about as chaotic as you'd imagine for a rainy Friday evening in the Big Apple. The triage area was full, and the hallway was lined with a train of gurneys holding people in various states of distress. I threaded my way through the mob to the nurses' station and gave the nurse on duty the name of the guy I was looking for. She scanned their computer records while I kept my fingers crossed and tried not to notice the walking wounded all around me. I'd seen enough animal gore for one day and was in no mood for the human wreckage.

My hunch proved right; he was there. *Good*, I thought. I was always glad when we got a really bad guy. I was looking forward to seeing this guy's case through to its end—with some jail time. I thought of the poor cat back at Bergh Memorial and hoped the doctors had been able to save him.

The nurse had directed me to the area where the cat's owner was, but there were several curtained-off areas, and I wasn't sure which one he was in. A doctor approached, and I described the patient I was looking for.

"Right there," he said, pointing to one of the curtains.

"What's his condition?" I asked.

"We just finished stitching him up," the doctor told me.

"Yeah, they told me he had a scratch," I said.

"Scratch? He's lucky he didn't lose an eye," the doctor said.

I agreed, although privately I was thinking he probably deserved whatever licks the poor cat had managed to get in before being bashed into a stupor. "Thanks," I said and was just about to go in when my cell phone rang.

I answered it quickly and hurried to find a relatively quiet area where I could talk without getting yelled at for having a cell phone in the hospital.

"This is Doctor Lanum," the voice on the other end said. She was one of the doctors who'd been caring for the cat I'd just brought in.

"Hi. How's the cat?" I asked, fearing the worst. I was sure she was calling to let me know the cat had died of his injuries. If so, it would be a hollow victory arresting this guy.

But the cat wasn't dead. I listened as she explained his condition to me.

"You have to be kidding," I said, stunned.

She repeated what she'd just told me.

"Wow," was all I could say.

"Thought you'd want to know," she said.

"Yep. Thanks for calling," I said and ended the call.

The truth is stranger than fiction, they say. I guess I would have to agree. Shaking my head in disbelief, I put my phone away and went in to talk to the owner of the cat.

"George Morrow?" I asked.

The truth is stranger than fiction, they say. I guess I would have to agree. Shaking my head in disbelief, I put my phone away and went in to talk to the owner of the cat.

"Yes?" He was older, probably in his late sixties, and he was handsome in a craggy way, with a red face and lots of wavy white hair. And, oh, yeah—his face looked like it had just been mauled by a lion.

"Hi. I'm Officer Salaks, from the ASPCA. Can I talk to you for a minute?"

"How's my cat?" were the first words out of his mouth. He sounded genuinely concerned.

"He's doing all right. But most important, how are you?" I asked him.

"I'm OK." He pointed to his head. "I got a few stitches is all."

I regarded his injuries for a moment. He had several nasty gashes on his face and head, five or six of them bristling with fresh black stitches, one long one under his Coke-bottle glasses and right over his eyelid—nearly thirty stitches in all. There were crusty patches of dried blood on his face and hands, and his clothes were as stained as the apartment had been.

"Can you tell me what happened, George?" I asked him.

"I just don't know," he said. "Blackie, my cat, was hissing at Piper, my other cat. I went over to see what that was about, and Blackie jumped on my head. I couldn't get him off me. He just wouldn't let go, so I grabbed the mallet and hit him. He finally jumped off me, and I was bleeding so much, I just came here." He gestured around him. "Doc says it's a good thing I was wearing my glasses or I could've lost my eye."

"Looks like you were lucky," I agreed.

"How's Blackie?" he asked again. "I didn't want to hit him, but he wouldn't let go."

I took a slow breath in and out. I'd had some time to get used to the idea, and I still could hardly believe it. "Blackie's fine," I told him. "When I found him in your apartment, it looked like he was injured. So I took him in to our animal hospital, and the doctors checked him out."

I filled him in on what I'd learned from Doctor Lanum. The cat's vitals were normal, the X-rays revealed no broken bones, *and there wasn't a scratch on him*—all that blood in the apartment had been George's!

If George really was a schizophrenic, he was taking his meds, and they were definitely working. I went on chatting with him for a while, and he seemed to be a perfectly nice, normal guy. He told me a little more about himself and his cats. He was sixty-eight years old. He'd had Blackie and Piper (I told him I hadn't noticed another cat; he told me Piper ran and hid under the bed when Blackie attacked George) since they were kittens. Blackie was ten, and Piper, an orange tabby, was nine. He said that Blackie had been having these hissing fits and that they'd started a couple of months before, but he hadn't paid

much attention to them. Most important, George Morrow talked like a guy who really loved his cats.

The next morning, I went to the hospital to check on Blackie. The cat seemed to be acting normal; the shock from the day before had apparently worn off. I found Doctor Lanum and told her what I'd learned about Blackie's behavior and the events of the day before.

"Well, from what you're telling me, it sounds like a meningioma," Doctor Lanum told me. She explained that Blackie's behavior fit the symptoms of a certain type of brain tumor.

Thinking of George, I asked if the condition was treatable, and she explained the procedure. Blackie would have to be put under general anesthesia while they did an MRI on his brain to determine whether the tumor was operable. In a large number of cases it would not be, and even if it were, the cost would be astronomical. There was no way a guy like George could even afford the MRI, much less the surgery. Left untreated, Blackie's aggressive behavior would probably continue and even worsen.

With great regret, I called George and gave him the bad news. Poor guy. He loved his cat but, of course, he couldn't afford the treatment and was worried that Blackie would really harm the other cat if he came home in that condition. He wasn't at all concerned about the potential danger to himself.

"What do you want to do, George?" I asked him.

His voice broke when he asked me to go ahead and have Blackie euthanized, and I wished I'd had the time to go over to tell him the news face to face, instead of over the phone.

When I did get a chance, I retrieved George's mallet from the safe and called him to tell him I was coming by to return it.

He had asked me about the mallet; he used it for woodworking, and there was no reason for us to hold it since this hadn't been a cruelty case after all. I returned the mallet, visited with George and Piper for a few minutes, and said good-bye.

On my way through the lobby, I ran into the woman who'd first reported the incident. "Hello, Officer. Are you here to take away that horrible man?" she asked.

"As a matter of fact, no," I told her.

"Uh, he hit his cat with a hammer. Aren't you supposed to do something about that?"

Her "holier than thou" tone was pissing me off. And I was annoyed with her for biasing me against the guy in the first place. I made a private vow: no matter what complainants or witnesses said, from then on I would never make up my mind that a suspect was a bad person until I'd weighed all the evidence myself.

"He did hit the cat. But the cat was attacking him at the time. Did you know he had nearly thirty stitches and almost lost an eye? I'd call that more than just a scratch, wouldn't you?"

"You're not doing your job. You should have arrested him," she told me.

I started to make a retort but held my tongue and just walked past her.

"Shame on you for not doing your job," she called after me. "It's animal cruelty!"

I turned to look at her before I left the building. I thought of George and his surviving cat, and Blackie, and all that blood. "It was self-defense," I told her firmly, then pushed through the door an walked out.

Another case closed.

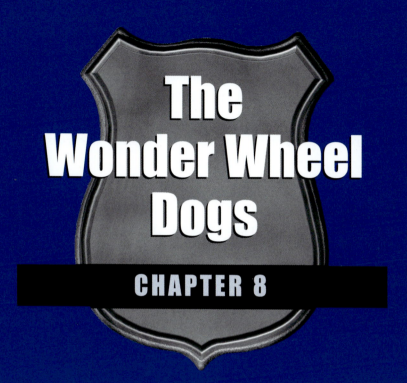

The Wonder Wheel Dogs

CHAPTER 8

No matter where you're from, the word *summertime* probably brings to mind the same images: that feeling of freedom when school is out; bike riding or skateboarding or hiding out in the shade of a tree house; the tinkle of music heralding the ice cream or snow cone man, and the taste of the cold sweetness on your tongue; the smell of hot asphalt blistering in the heat, or the drone of a mower and the sharp scent of freshly cut grass. For some, summertime means amusement parks. If you grew up anywhere near New York or its five boroughs, it means Coney Island.

When I got the call from Base requesting my location and then directing me to check out a complaint at Coney Island, I was skeptical. Animals at an amusement park? "What's the nature of the complaint?" I radioed back.

"Be advised, we received a call from a complainant stating that two dogs were riding the Ferris wheel at Coney Island," Base responded.

Envisioning that, I let out a snort of disbelieving laughter. I thought I'd heard wrong, or that someone in the office was joking around, trying to play a trick on me. "Base, can you repeat that?" I asked, turning up the volume on my radio just to make sure I was hearing correctly.

"Caller stated that there were two dogs riding the Ferris wheel at Coney Island."

Although the dispatcher's voice was perfectly calm, I couldn't help laughing out loud. Dogs riding a Ferris wheel? Either the complainant was crazy, or this I had to see.

I got a hold of myself long enough to sound serious for a minute. "10-4, Base, will check care and condition." Then, still giggling at the thought, I drove toward Coney Island.

I used to work for the New York City Parks Department, in the Mounted Unit. Once, they sent us to Coney Island to patrol the beaches during a period when there was a lifeguard shortage. From the beach, I could see the park through the shimmering heat waves. Every once in a while, the wind would carry the rumble of the Cyclone, the big old wooden roller coaster, and the shrieks of the people riding it to where I was patrolling. But because I was working, I never had a chance to actually go inside the park.

When I got the call from Base … directing me to check out a complaint at Coney Island, I was skeptical. Animals at an amusement park? "What's the nature of the complaint?" I radioed back.

I left my car on nearby Neptune Avenue and walked toward the park. A fish-and-salt-smelling ocean breeze was holding its own against the heat. It was a weekday, and still pretty early, so Astroland, as the amusement park is actually named, wasn't officially open yet. At the time, I'd been in New York for fifteen years and had never visited the amusement park. I was looking forward to finally seeing the place without having to battle the crowds.

The Ferris wheel is easy to spot. At 150 feet tall, it is the most enormous structure there, towering over even the Cyclone. And in case you're still having trouble finding it, right in the middle of the wheel, it says WONDER WHEEL in red neon letters, six feet high. But finding the entrance to the place was another matter.

The first gate I came to was closed. After some circling, I finally came across a paved walkway that led down an incline to the area where you board the Wonder Wheel. Near this entrance, I spotted a large wooden doghouse inside a fenced area easily big enough for four dogs. *Guess I'm on the right trail,* I thought to myself.

I pulled out my camera and stepped up to the enclosure to photograph the area. That's when the two German Shepherd Dogs appeared. They popped out of the doghouse and ran toward me, tails wagging, barking an excited greeting. They were big and gorgeous, with clean, healthy coats and good body weights. I noticed a few big steel bowls for food and water. Obviously, these dogs were well cared for. Glancing around at the heat waves shimmering off the concrete, it occurred to me that this lower-level entrance area was probably the best place to house the dogs; it was the shadiest spot on the lot.

I took a few photos and called out, "Is anyone here?"

"Can I help you?" asked a man who appeared from behind the enclosure.

"Hi. I'm looking for the owner of these dogs," I told him.

"That's me," he replied.

When I told him why I was there, he started to laugh. "Yep," he said, nodding, "it happens a lot. People complain about the dogs riding." He glanced at me, taking in my uniform. "It's been a while, but you guys have been here before."

He rested his arms on the fence and gestured to the dogs. "Yesterday it got pretty hot, and the dogs were down here in the house. They started barking, so I knew they wanted to go on."

"Go on?" I prompted. This I had to hear.

He nodded and again made a gesture to the dogs, which were sitting close by, looking relaxed, their attention on their owner. "I've raised these dogs since they were puppies. They've been here all their lives. I don't force them on. Sometimes it gets hot for them, and certain times of year the biting flies get bad, so they like to ride around and cool off."

I could believe that. After all, how many times have you seen a dog with his head sticking out a car window, obviously enjoying the rush of air? "You mean they ride the Wonder Wheel," I said, just to make sure.

"Yep. I'll show you." He went to the gate and started to unlock it. "Right now, we're doing some maintenance on the Wonder Wheel, so it's off, but I'll open the gate and show you I don't have to coax them into the car."

The dogs were waiting by the gate, quiet and alert. When he swung it open I had to smile. The way the dogs bolted out the gate reminded me of a horse race, and I couldn't help saying "Aaaaand they're off!"

We followed a few quick strides behind, and I saw the dogs zip up the ramp to the Wonder Wheel and jump into an open car. No force was used, or even voice commands. The door remained open, and dogs stayed inside. After a minute, when nothing happened, they started to bark as if to say, "Hey, what's the holdup? Let's get going here!"

The owner chuckled. "See?" he said. "They think they're going for a ride. They've been doing this for years. They bark when they want to ride, and they bark when they want to get off."

The dogs looked so German-Shepherd-demanding and puppy-dog-hopeful at the same time, I had to laugh, too. They stayed in the car while I continued to chat with the owner. Most of the cars on the Wonder Wheel glide back and forth on tracks as the wheel turns; the dogs rode in one of the eight stationary cars (all are enclosed, bucket-style cars). When they

> *We followed a few quick strides behind, and I saw the dogs zip up the ramp to the Wonder Wheel and jump into an open car. No force was used, or even voice commands.*

were riding high, the air was at least ten degrees cooler up there, a real blessing in the heat. The owner even kept bowls of food and water in the car for the dogs. Although the dogs were obviously healthy, protocol said I had to inquire about veterinary care. That was all on the up-and-up, too; the guy's sister was a veterinarian, and she looked after them. I thanked the man and told him I was closing out the complaint. There was no animal cruelty there.

As I strolled back to my car, I smiled, picturing the dogs riding the Wonder Wheel. I promised myself I would come back sometime when it was working and see them in action. Then I thought of something else. He must lose a lot of money in the busy summer season with one car reserved for the dogs. Obviously, that wasn't important to him. Keeping his dogs happy was. In my book, he was the kind of dog owner you really like.

Later, when I had finished writing up my cases for the day, I called back the complainant on the Wonder Wheel dogs. I wanted to let her know that we had indeed followed up on the complaint and reassure her that there was no cruelty in this case. As it turned out, this individual worked for a well-known animal welfare organization. She hadn't actually seen the dogs herself but had been informed by someone else that the dogs were riding the Ferris wheel. I assured her that the dogs were in excellent condition and explained the situation to her.

"Well, I don't think that's right. It's not safe," she said indignantly. "Just because the dogs seem to like it doesn't mean he should let them ride."

"In this case, it would be cruel *not* to let them ride," I wanted to say, but didn't. No matter what I said, it wasn't going to make this woman happy.

"You can bet I'm going to get the media involved in this," she threatened.

"That's your prerogative," I told her politely.

Still incensed at my failure to take her side, she hung up the phone. As far as I know, no media coverage resulted.

My boss and I talked about it later and agreed—you just can't please everybody. But I know a couple of German Shepherd Dogs at Coney Island that are easy to please!

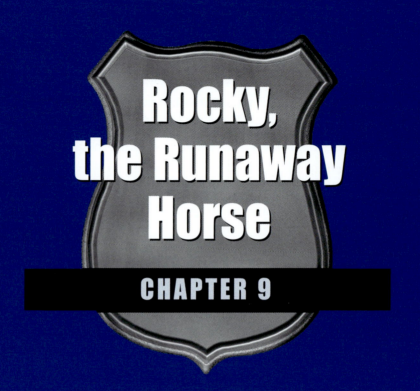

Rocky, the Runaway Horse

CHAPTER 9

Once a snowbird, always a snowbird. Some New Yorkers hate it, but where I grew up, the ground was often white from November to April. When the Big Apple freezes, I feel right at home.

I remember one snowy day in particular. Usually in inclement weather, our call load went through the roof, but this wasn't a storm. This was movie set snow: a gentle white drifting that fell like feathers, covering the grit and grime and decorating the bare branches of the trees. It seemed to have a soothing effect on the whole city. The phones at headquarters had been quiet, and I had finished my cases early. I decided to check on the carriage horses in Central Park.

There are hack lines, or hack stands, where the carriages line up to wait for hire, at a few different locations in or near the park, mostly along Central Park South. There you'll see a line of anywhere from five to more than a dozen fancy horse-drawn carriages for hire, mostly by tourists who want to see Central Park the old-fashioned way. If the weather gets too hot (90 degrees) or too cold (below 18 degrees), the horses by law are not allowed out of the stables. But other than that, you'll see them out in all kinds of weather, just like the tourists. The ASPCA periodically inspects the hack lines to check on the condition of the horses and to make sure that no drivers are trying to buck the temperature rules by working their horses in extreme conditions.

I entered the park at Ninetieth Street, then made my way across the transverse to the West Side and down to Central Park South. I counted about fifteen horses in the hack line there, looking like a perfect replica of a Currier and Ives Christmas card, with their bright plumes and shiny harnesses and the snow falling all around. They were all blanketed to keep off the chill while they waited for hire, and some were munching grain from plastic buckets. Nothing seemed amiss. All in all, it was a peaceful scene.

I should have known it wouldn't last.

At the Sixth Avenue entrance, I turned onto Central Park Drive and headed north. I was cruising along, enjoying the snowy scenery, but I noticed that the drives hadn't been plowed yet. A couple of inches had accumulated, which would make for slippery conditions for the horses. Up ahead, I spotted a hired carriage and slowed down, looking carefully to see how the horse was handling the snowy footing. When I worked for the Parks Department Mounted Unit, our horses were always shod with little boreum cleats in the winter to give extra traction. They also had special pads on their shoes—a shod horse's foot in the snow acts like a big scoop, mounding the snow into slippery balls of ice. The pads pop the snow out with every step. Carriage horses aren't required to have these special shoes, however, because they travel only on roadways that are supposed to be plowed. If the horses were out on these unplowed roads, they wouldn't be trotting, they'd be skating.

I stopped and watched carefully as the carriage drew closer, but the horse didn't appear to be having any trouble with the footing. Twenty yards behind the horse and carriage, however, was a little green Parks Department truck pushing a snowplow down the drive. The driver of the truck slowed down to pass the carriage. The horse trotted a few steps, nervous about the plow, but then relaxed as the truck went on its way.

I drove on, past Wollman Rink and down the drive that backs the Central Park Zoo. At the Fifth Avenue hack stand, there were only a couple of horses. They looked fine. I circled the perimeter and came back into the park at Tavern on the Green. Near there, on the West Drive, I spotted another carriage. Just then, I was waved over by a park patron asking for directions. I pointed out the best route to Bethesda Fountain, and when I looked again, another little green snowplow truck, or maybe the same one, was trolling down the drive going the same direction as the carriage. As before, the truck driver slowed down to pass the carriage, and this horse shied, too, scooting forward on the slippery streets before coming back to a quick nervous walk, swinging its head left and right, trying to see around its blinkers.

Although horses in general will spook at large noisy objects, the carriage horses are used to being surrounded by trucks, cars, cabs, and the busy honking rush of ongoing traffic. To see one horse spook at a snowplow truck wasn't unusual. Maybe that horse had never encountered one before. But seeing two horses spook made me uneasy. The truck hadn't been all that noisy, and it wasn't the first snow of the year.

I continued my circuit of the park and soon reached the small loop, part of the most common route for the carriages. I was on a section of the loop referred to as the zoo drive, which I noticed had been plowed. I stopped yet again to give directions, then took a minute to update my memo book. I was just finishing my entries, when I happened to look up and see a horse and carriage moving quite a bit faster than it should have. I hit the windshield wipers to get a better look, and he kept cantering on.

Carriage horses are permitted to walk and trot *only*. A cantering carriage horse in these conditions was definitely cause for concern.

I spotted the horse barreling down the drive. The afternoon light was waning, and the snow was still coming down. I peered through the swirling flakes trying to make out the driver of the carriage, then felt a chill that had nothing to do with the weather: there was no driver. The carriage was a runaway!

A spooked horse will bolt for the nearest place it feels safe. Usually, that's home. In this case, home would be the hack stables:

west on Central Park South and down Seventh or Ninth Avenue to the thirties, forties, or fifties where the stables were, then another block or two over past Ninth or Tenth Avenue. Horses know the way home. But it was more than a mile through the icy streets—and it was nearly rush hour. I had to try to stop the horse before it got out of the park and ran into traffic.

The drive in that area of the park has three lanes: two for official vehicles, and one for the carriage horses. Sections of concrete median three or four feet wide separate the lanes to keep vehicles from accidentally veering into the carriage lane. The horse was cantering down the carriage lane, less than forty yards away and closing fast. The easiest way to stop him would be to block the carriage lane with my squad car. There were throughways between the medians to allow official vehicles access when necessary. Unfortunately, the plowed snow was piled deep enough to hide the throughways. The horse was coming fast; I had only seconds to make a decision. If I'd had a four-wheel drive vehicle, I could've driven over the median no problem. But in my car, in the snow, driving over a curb would be a bad idea. Should I turn around and try to race the horse back to the throughway nearest the park entrance? If I got there before he did, with enough time to maneuver, I could block the entrance with my squad car, forcing the horse to stop—if I could find the throughway. But what if I didn't get into position in time?

My other option was to try to stop the runaway horse immediately, right where I was. For one more second I considered, then decided I might not beat him to the park entrance. It was now or never. I jumped out of my squad car and ran out into the carriage lane.

I could block the entrance with my squad car, forcing the horse to stop—if I could find the throughway. But what if I didn't get into position in time?

The drive took a definite downhill slope at that point, and the frightened horse began to pick up speed. I had to stop him, but if the horse stopped too fast, I was afraid he would go into a skid. He might stumble, or even worse, flip the carriage. The horse was about twenty yards away now, still heading straight toward me at a pretty good clip. I began waving my arms to try to get his attention and called out "Whoa, boy—whooooooa," in the most convincing tone I could muster.

The gap closed. Ten yards. Eight. I stood my ground. "Whoa, boy," I called again. Three yards. I was waving wildly now. One yard. "Whoa!" I yelled one last time. It was no use. He wasn't stopping. I jumped aside at the last second and watched helplessly as the horse cantered on toward Fifth Avenue. Worse, as the carriage passed I could see it wasn't empty after all. There was no driver, but in the velvet-lined backseat were two passengers: I had one quick glimpse of a young couple clutching each other, their faces frozen in terror as the carriage whizzed by.

"Oh, no!" I said out loud.

Two older women who happened to be walking down the drive had witnessed the whole thing. "You don't know a thing about horses," one of them said.

Never let it be said that New Yorkers are not helpful.

Several responses came to mind, but this was no time for quips. I held my tongue and ran for my car. The carriage was heading straight for the Grand Army Plaza, a busy loop near the heavily trafficked intersection of Fifth Avenue and Fifty-ninth Street. I started the car, flipped on my lights (no siren—that would just spook him more), and headed down the zoo drive after the carriage.

I was seconds behind as the horse reached the end of the drive. The same two carriages I had seen earlier were still parked at the hack stand. Beyond was Grand Army Plaza, Fifth Avenue, and the already heavy pre–rush hour traffic.

Horses act on instinct. One of the strongest ones is the herd instinct. I held my breath and prayed that the horse would run to his buddies at the hack stand and stop there. The alternative was the run-for-home instinct, which would result in the horse galloping straight through the Grand Army Plaza into the middle of Fifth Avenue.

The light changed. The traffic lurched forward. The speeding carriage hit the street.

"Don't get hit, don't get hit," I repeated out loud, since all I could do at that point was cross my fingers and will the horse to stop.

Miraculously, the traffic cleared. The horse ran to the hack stand and stopped with "the herd." I pulled up right behind him.

One of the carriage drivers, an old Irish guy named Stanley, caught the horse by the bridle and held him.

"What happened?" Stanley asked, as I jumped out of the car and hurried up to him.

"I'm not sure," I told him and explained how I'd encountered the runaway.

Then I remembered the passengers. "Are you OK?" I asked, peering over the side of the carriage.

"Yeah, I think so," the guy managed to answer. The poor couple looked completely stunned. Slowly, they let go of each other and sat up.

"Are you sure?" I asked.

"Yeah, we're fine," he answered in a more normal voice. "But that was crazy."

"I just want to get out," the woman said shakily.

They climbed out and stood by the carriage while I checked the horse's condition. He didn't appear to be injured, although he was still breathing hard from the long run. It's a good thing the incident hadn't happened in the hot weather, or the horse's condition after such a wild gallop might have been really serious.

I thought I recognized the horse. "This is Rocky, isn't it?" I asked Stanley.

He nodded. I knew Rocky's owner; he had a few horses and a few different drivers working for him. Stanley didn't know which driver was using Rocky that day.

I was just about to call Rocky's owner when I saw a bulky figure hustling toward us down the zoo drive. It was Alberto, the missing driver.

Alberto is not what you'd call the athletic type. By the time he caught up, he was huffing and puffing so hard I was afraid he'd have a heart attack. He was also bundled up like the Michelin tire man.

"Rocky's fine, Alberto," I answered his questioning look. He was so winded he couldn't speak. "Are you OK?"

He nodded, explaining between gasps, "I'm OK. I ran most of the loop trying to catch him."

"What happened?" I asked, when he'd caught his breath. I was dying to know how Alberto and Rocky had parted company.

"I got a fare," he told us, with a gesture toward the couple, "and I helped them into the carriage. I started to climb up, and this little green truck came by."

The snowplow again!

"Rocky spooked and took off, and I got knocked off."

He was an older guy. I was still kind of worried about him, especially since he'd just told me he fell off the carriage when Rocky bolted. "Are you sure you're not hurt?" I asked him.

He shook his head. "I knew it was going to snow," he explained, "so I wore two snowsuits today." He grinned and pointed at his bulky attire.

"So you had plenty of padding." I laughed. "Good thinking." An older tourist couple strolling by stopped with an interested look at the carriages. I thought of the snowplow trucks and Rocky's mad dash through the park.

"Listen, guys," I said to Alberto and the other drivers. "I don't know why all the horses are spooking at the snowplows today, but I'm not going to see this happen again. I'm suspending all the horses from service."

Sometimes the drivers get annoyed when the ASPCA suspends them, but this time nobody said a word. I guess they had no trouble understanding how dangerous the runaway situation was and how lucky we all were that it had ended happily. And I'm sure each driver was relieved that it hadn't happened to him.

The shaken couple moved on, looking as if they needed a stiff drink to calm their nerves. I offered to follow Alberto and Rocky back to the stable, but Stanley said he would go with them—in front, so Rocky couldn't run away again. I thanked him for looking after his fellow driver.

"Be sure to put some Bigeloil on Rocky's legs," I called out to Alberto as they started home. Bigeloil is like Ben-Gay for horses. I figured Rocky was going to be sore after his unintentional workout.

I made the rounds of the other hack lines again, this time sending all the drivers in. Then I called all the stables and warned them not to send out any more horses. While I was writing everything up in my memo book, I got a call from Rocky's owner, who had just heard the whole story. He wanted me to know that he had left word for his drivers that he didn't want his horses out that day, but Alberto hadn't gotten the message. He thanked me for helping, and we shared a chuckle over how horses will suddenly decide to be afraid of something they've seen dozens of times.

Oh, those little green trucks.

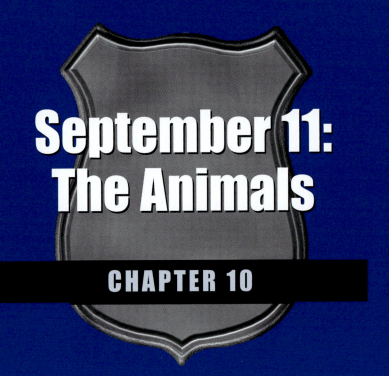

September 11: The Animals

CHAPTER 10

She is huddled in the farthest corner of the room, behind the bed. It seems like the safest place, although really she thinks nowhere can be safe. She doesn't know how long she's been there; dimly, she's conscious of passing hours, marked by physical urges: hunger, thirst, and sleep; once, shakily, she crept out of the corner and peed on the floor, too frightened to leave the bedroom. She's too warm; there's no air conditioning, no open windows. She thinks of going to the kitchen for water but can't bring herself to leave the corner again. Such paralyzing fear she has never known.

• • •

September 11, 2001. There are not enough words in all the languages of the world to describe the sorrow brought about by what happened that day. I know. I was there. I saw the aftermath and heard, ate, slept, and literally breathed it: the burning pile of wreckage, the rescuers, the heroes, and the scoundrels. I saw the hope turn to grief on the faces of the victims' families and grieved with them and the rest of the world as we all realized that no one was coming out of that pile alive.

I don't have to tell you how courageous the rescue workers were who tried to save the people trapped in the World Trade Center towers in the minutes before they fell. I have the deepest admiration for them, and for the ones who searched the wreckage afterward looking for survivors. The whole world wanted to help them, including me, but my job on those dark days was to search for another kind of victim: the animals that had been left behind.

· · ·

The tense minutes of sleep, when they come, are a relief. Awake, she is in a state of low-level panic, remembering over and over the events of the day before—the noise: engine sounds, too loud, too close, and then a slamming and silence. Instinct tells her to freeze. She waits, understanding something very bad is about to happen, is happening, has happened. The windows are closed, the apartment far above street level, but slowly another noise begins, and in the quiet apartment she hears it very clearly: the sound of people screaming. Agitated, she scrambles toward the front door, freezes again, darts forward, freezes, instinct having failed her. Finally, she bolts into the bedroom and finds the corner. Soon there is another sound, a terrible sound, a rumble that builds to a whining roar that tortures her ears and shakes her, shakes the room, shakes the air itself, and seems to suck it out of her lungs. Frantic, she runs in a circle, cries out, lunges for the bed, and goes back to the corner, cowering there until that noise subsides. When it happens again, she flinches, whimpers, and flattens herself against the floor. She shuts her eyes tight against the terror as the apartment slowly darkens and the dust and an evil smell of burning fill the air.

• • •

In the midst of that immense tragedy, there were countless smaller tragedies involving those who were still alive. Thousands of people who lived near the World Trade Center left their homes in the morning and weren't allowed back in. Hundreds more were forced to evacuate their homes with no notice and no way to transport anything but a small bag of belongings and the clothes on their backs. They left quickly, thinking they'd be back in a couple of days. Many put out supplies of food and water for their pets and left them behind, thinking they'd be better off. No one thought it would turn out to be several days, weeks, and in some cases, months before they were allowed to return to their homes.

And then there were those who never came home.

• • •

Come daylight, she is still alone. She knows she is alone, and a low moan escapes her throat, rising to a howl of anguish.

• • •

The morning of September 12, I was up at dawn. In fact, I had hardly slept all night. I left my house early that morning wearing sneakers, certain I would be walking a couple of miles across town to get to the ASPCA offices on the East Side. I was surprised to find the crosstown bus running.

I was one of three ASPCA agents who made it in to work that day. If you lived in Manhattan, you could at least count on walking wherever you needed to go. Some of the buses and trains were running. But people living outside the city couldn't get in at all, either by driving or via public transportation.

I came into an eerily quiet headquarters. The three of us greeted each other quietly, the same way most New Yorkers greeted each other in the days that followed the attacks on the World Trade Center: a polite good morning, then the careful inquiry, "How's your family? Is everyone you know OK?"

We didn't go out on our regular rounds that day to check out cruelty complaints. Instead, we manned the phones. I think we logged more than 200 calls that first day, all reports of animals left alone, either because the owners were missing or because they'd evacuated the area and found they couldn't get back home to their pets. Dozens of times that day, I recorded the stories of tearful callers and tried not to cry myself. Most went something like this:

Salaks: HLE. This is Agent Salaks.

Caller (male voice): Yes, I'm calling about a dog [pause].

Salaks: Yes? What is wrong with the dog?

Caller: He's alone. He's locked in the apartment. He's . . . [muffled sound].

Salaks: Are you the owner of the dog?

Caller: No. No, I'm . . . it's my . . . my brother's dog. My brother is . . . missing [caller's voice breaking]. I'm sorry . . . [long pause]. Can you help?

I spent most of that day reassuring callers that animals are resilient, that they would be OK for a couple of days, longer if they had water. I just wished I could have offered callers the same reassurance about their missing friends and loved ones.

. . .

When she can no longer give voice to her loneliness, she becomes quiet again. She thinks of Them. She will wait—wait for Them. Waiting is a job she knows how to do, and this calms her.

. . .

While we were taking calls, ASPCA management was in the process of coordinating with the Office of Emergency Management (OEM) to figure out some sort of procedure for rescuing the abandoned animals. I knew that it takes time and careful planning to work out the details of such a huge operation. But for me, it was torture sitting in that office all day as the list of pets in need of help grew longer and longer, and all I could do was answer the phones.

. . .

She sits up to change position, then settles down again. Her eyes and nasal passages feel seared from the stench and the bad air. She is very thirsty. Her throat aches with the thirst and the loneliness.

. . .

The next day, a few more agents were able to make it in to ASPCA headquarters. As quickly as we could, we packed up some supplies and headed downtown. Our Care-A-Van (a big RV the ASPCA uses as a mobile animal clinic), manned by our veterinary hospital staff, led the way, followed by ASPCA vehicles driven by a skeleton crew of the five of us who'd managed to get in to work. We weren't sure what to expect. We just knew that there was a long list of people hoping to get to their beloved pets, and we were going to do our best to help them.

We just knew that there was a long list of people hoping to get to their beloved pets, and we were going to do our best to help them.

For the past two days, I'd had a knot in my stomach worrying about the victims, both people and animals. It was a relief to finally be doing something, but as I drove down the deserted FDR Drive, I realized the knot wasn't going away. If anything, as we approached the disaster area, it was getting worse.

For days, even people miles uptown and upwind of Ground Zero could smell the acrid smoke from the burning pile. As we drew closer to the site, the cloud of smoke billowing from it loomed ominously overhead, and the smell became something indescribable. They say your sense of smell is the strongest of all your senses. I'm no scientist, but I know that even after all this time I can still smell it. It's indelibly recorded in my brain.

Our base of operations was Pier 40 on the Hudson River, about three-quarters of a mile from Ground Zero. When we pulled in, the area was thronged with workers, donated supplies, and distraught people waiting anxiously for word about how they were going to get to their pets. We assembled for muster and were given specific instructions. We would be supplied with extra flashlights and batteries since the buildings we'd be going into were without power. We were told to shower at the end of a shift, no matter how tired we were. And we were given gas masks—not the big heavy-duty ones that make you look like an alien, but a smaller version that still looked weird and made me uneasy. For the first time, I wondered what the health risks of this job were going to be. Then I told myself there was no use worrying about it. Plenty of people—and animals—were down there breathing the same air and suffering a lot more than I was. I put it out of my mind and went to pick up my flashlights and batteries from the pile of supplies.

We started that morning at Battery Park City, a group of condominiums that form a community almost directly across from Ground Zero. We were working with the Parks Department as well as volunteers from the Nassau County Sheriff's Department and a couple of humane organizations. Some of the higher-ups had decided that a group effort would be best, so we loaded up the dozen or so vehicles we had with pet carriers and anxious owners and set out in a convoy.

My first trip was with a young woman who said hello, got into the back of my Chevy Blazer, and started to sob.

I handed her a tissue and gave her a few moments. "I'm Tina," I said. "What's your name?"

"Suzanne," she managed to get out.

"Suzanne, it's going to be OK." This poor girl was so upset; I just wanted to help her calm down. "Do you have a dog or a cat?" I asked her.

"Two dogs," she said.

"What kind?"

"Jack Russell Terriers," she said, sounding calmer.

"What're their names?" I prompted.

"Louie and Marty. I just want to get them out," she said, and started sobbing all over again.

"Hey, we're going to get them out. That's what we're going to do, right now," I reassured her. I passed her another tissue and waited until she quieted down again.

She blew her nose and took a deep breath. "You're not from New York, are you?"

"No. How could you tell?"

"You're nice," she said. "And you don't talk like a New Yorker."

"Neither do you," I said, deciding to ignore the first part. "Where're you from?"

"Nebraska," she said. "You?"

"I'm a 'cheese-head,'" I told her. "Wisconsin. How long have you been in New York?"

"I just moved here two months ago. I had a job offer . . . it seemed like such a great opportunity. . . ." She made a helpless gesture that seemed to mean *until all this happened.*

My heart went out to her. She was young, probably right out of college. Two months wasn't nearly enough time for a laid-back midwesterner to adjust to the crazy pace of New York—and then to have terrorists attack practically on top of where you live. She went on to tell me that she had no family here and no real friends as of yet. Her dogs were all she had, and she wasn't sure what had happened to them in the two days since she had been away.

"Hey, it's going to be OK," I told her. "We're going to get your dogs out." I hoped I was right.

As we approached Battery Park City, I got my first look at the area around Ground Zero and felt a shiver go down my spine. The site itself was blocked from our view by the buildings still standing around it, but we were just a few hundred yards away, and the smoke and smell pervaded everything. The air was hazy, and everything around was covered with a gray film of ashy dust. Debris from the collapse—unidentifiable pieces of stuff as well as papers and random items like framed photographs—littered the area. Weaving around the larger clumps, we pulled into a parking area in Battery Park City.

I think all of us were sort of dazed. We got out of the cars slowly, assaulted by the visual chaos and the stench. The place was decimated, and this was an area where the buildings had not suffered any real structural damage. Staring disbelievingly at the destruction, we discussed last-minute instructions, then began escorting our passengers to their buildings to rescue their pets.

Suzanne and I cautiously entered the lobby of her building and started down the hall toward the stairway. The deeper into the building we went, the darker it became, and I had the sensation that we were walking into a cave. We had to turn on our flashlights before we'd gone fifty feet. The red carpet was coated with the same powder-fine dust that had fallen elsewhere, and in the beams of the flashlights, we could see the dust stirring up into the air with every step.

"Put your mask on," I reminded her, pulling my own mask over my nose and mouth. I didn't even want to think about what the dust might consist of; whatever it was, I knew we didn't want to be breathing it.

We found the stairway and started up, our feet echoing loudly on the concrete steps. "What floor do you live on?" I asked her.

"The ninth," she said.

"Well, that's not too bad," I said, thinking of the twenty-something floors many of these buildings had.

By the fifth floor, I had to stop.

"What's the matter?" Suzanne asked me.

I shook my head. "This mask. Something's not working right." I felt like I wasn't getting any air. I took it off and repositioned it. "It's OK. Let's go."

We started up the stairs again, but after two more flights, I was getting lightheaded from oxygen deprivation. Clearly, these masks weren't meant for intense physical exertion. In disgust, I pulled it off and hung it around my neck. I was now breathing the dust, but at least I could breathe.

We trudged up four more flights and at last reached the ninth floor. Once there, I paused to check in by radio as we'd been instructed to do, but the only response was a steady, lifeless crackle. The unblinking red indicator light told me there was no signal. All the transmitters had been knocked out when the area lost power.

Looks like we're on our own, I thought. *I hope nothing goes wrong . . .*

I was now following Suzanne down the winding hallway. She flashed her light on the apartment doors, checking numbers, and I kept my light trained on the floor ahead.

"Here it is," she said, indicating a door. She had pulled her own mask off by that time. She took out her keys and started to unlock the door. Then she hesitated, looking at me.

Once there, I paused to check in by radio as we'd been instructed to do, but the only response was a steady, lifeless crackle. The unblinking red indicator light told me there was no signal.

"Go ahead," I told her. "It's going to be OK."

She turned the key and pushed open the door. Before the door was open all the way, our flashlight beams caught two very happy Jack Russell Terriers streaking toward us. Somehow, despite all the licking and jumping and hugging, I managed to herd Suzanne and her dogs into the apartment and close the door behind us. I didn't know who was happier, Suzanne or the two dogs. I was smiling with relief, too, but I couldn't forget where we were.

"Suzanne, we need to get going," I told her. "Let's give them some water real quick, then we have to get out of here."

She got up immediately, and the dogs and I followed her to the kitchen. "Just water," I told her, "no food. They can eat after the vet checks them out." I tried the kitchen tap, and it was working. We filled the dogs' dishes and they lapped gratefully.

"Let me get their leashes," Suzanne said.

"That's fine. You may also want to grab a few other things," I suggested.

She gave me a puzzled look.

"A few clothes, your credit cards, cell phone charger. It may be a while before you're able to get back in here." Although she still looked shaken, she seemed to understand and went off to the bedroom. Her mind must've been going in circles, so I was trying to help her think ahead a little bit; I know I would have wanted someone to do the same for me.

A few minutes later, she returned with a small duffle bag. We leashed the dogs and started back the way we had come. Both gravity and anxiety sent us down the stairs and out of the building a lot faster than we'd gone up. I can't say we felt much more secure once we were out of the building, but at least there was light.

Back at the pier, the other agents and I dropped off our passengers along with their pets and prepared to make another run. Before I could pull away, Suzanne leaned in through my open window and gave me a big hug.

"I don't know how I can ever thank you," she said tearfully.

"You don't have to," I said. "This is my job."

She nodded, still teary eyed.

"Hey, Suzanne, I hope things work out for you. I know it's hard to believe this right now, but New York's really a great place. Take it from a fellow midwesterner."

She smiled a little through her tears, and the last I saw of her, she was leading Louie and Marty to the ASPCA's Care-A-Van. It was a great feeling knowing I'd helped her get her dogs out, but she was only the first one. There were hundreds more waiting. I hurried over to the main check-in area to pick up my next case.

All day we drove people to Battery Park City, escorted them into their apartments, and delivered them safely back to the Pier 40 checkpoint. Battery Park City was close; you could actually see it from the pier. It should have been a straight shot down the West Side Highway, an easy five-minute ride. But the highway had become a parking lot for all the emergency response teams and television crews. As a result, although Battery Park City was less than a mile south, to get there we had to go all the way east across Houston Street, then down and around the southern tip of Manhattan and back through the Battery Park underpass. All along the way, there were roadblocks, detours, and security checks. Sometimes we encountered caravans of rescue trucks with lights blazing and sirens wailing. Some one-way streets were now two-way, some of them were reversed, and many street signs were unreadable. Often the trip took more than an hour.

All day, we trudged up and down stairs in dark stuffy buildings. Many of the apartments were on floors numbering into the twenties; after a few trips like that, your quads are burning so much that there's not much difference between two flights and twenty. The masks we'd been issued proved to be useless in those conditions, so most of us simply went without. By midmorning, my eyes were red and burning, and I'd developed a nagging little cough that wouldn't go away.

Late in the afternoon, I went to pick up my next assignment and was told, "No one's going in right now."

"What's going on?" I asked.

"I don't know. OEM has everything frozen down there. They're not letting anyone in." Later we learned that President

Bush was on the scene at Ground Zero, and the Secret Service had shut everything down. It was good to be able to rest for a while, but as the minutes dragged on, then turned into hours, I grew more and more impatient. The longer we waited, the longer those stranded animals were stuck without food or water.

• • •

She is waiting, waiting. Her thirst is a constant burn in her throat.

• • •

When we finally started up again, it was getting dark. I will never forget how the southern tip of Manhattan looked with most of the buildings without power. Instead of the beautiful sparkling skyline dominated by the Twin Towers, lower Manhattan was a mass of dark buildings silhouetted against the glowing sky. The only light came from street level: the glare of emergency lights powered by generators as the rescue workers went doggedly on, searching through the pile.

On my last trip down that day, I was driving a very nice couple who were hoping to get their dog out. They'd been waiting most of the day before their turn came, and they were tired and anxious but so relieved to finally have their chance to go after their pet.

This time we weren't going to Battery Park City. Their building was in a different area, only two blocks from Ground Zero, in a restricted zone.

I'd been working for fourteen hours by then and thought I'd gotten used to everything. But when we came out of the Battery tunnel, we were all stunned.

The roar of so many big generators powering the emergency floodlights was deafening. And the stench of the burning pile just about smacked you in the face. It truly looked like a war zone, something like the glimpses of war-torn countries that you see on the news: crumbled mounds of dust-covered wreckage lit by the floodlights, and people in uniform hurrying back and forth, shouting orders above the chaos. The National Guard was on the scene. Soldiers with AK-47 semi-automatic rifles were posted on every corner, and military vehicles zoomed back and forth.

I parked the Blazer, and we got out and started down the block toward the couple's building. We hadn't gone twenty feet before a police sergeant stopped us. "Where are you going?" he demanded. He sounded so suspicious; I could hardly blame him. Everyone down there had been working for days in this living nightmare. Now that it was dark, everything and every-one seemed more of a threat.

I told him the address and explained what we were doing, and he gave me a nod and let us pass. But when we reached the corner of the block where the building was, we were stopped once again.

This time it was a National Guard soldier. He stepped for-ward, blocking our path, and confronted us, his gun at the ready. "This is a restricted area," he said in a military monotone. "No one goes in."

Once again I explained who we were and why we needed to be allowed in. "I don't know anything about that," he told me. "What I do know is this is a restricted zone."

"Please," the woman begged him. "We're just trying to get our dog out. She's been in there without food or water for days."

"Sorry ma'am. This is a restricted area," he replied.

The stench of the burning pile smacked you in the face. It looked like a war zone, something like the glimpses of war-torn countries that you see on the news.

Now the man spoke up. "Come on, guy," he said. "We'll just run up and get her quick and get out of your way." He tried a winning smile.

The soldier shifted his wide-legged stance and looked away toward the end of the block. He didn't speak—he didn't have to. Clearly there was no way we were getting by him.

"Come on," I said quietly to the couple. "We'll have to try again tomorrow."

We drove back to the pier in silence. I know how bitterly disappointing it was for the couple to have waited all day and come so close, only to be told they couldn't get their dog out.

I made my final check-in and reported the incident to my boss. These things were bound to happen with so many different agencies involved. We both hoped it was just a temporary situation, a lack of communication between OEM and the National Guard, because surely that couple's dog would not be the only animal stranded in a restricted zone.

It was after 10:00 by then, time to pack it in for the day. By that time, I'd been on the job for fifteen hours, yet I had mixed feelings about leaving the pier. I was incredibly tired, but at the same time I felt guilty going home when there were still so many people and animals in need of help.

. . .

By the third night, her thirst no longer allows her to sleep. She must have water. Driven by that need, she slowly uncurls herself from the corner and gets to her feet. Her muscles tremble, and walking requires all her attention. She makes it to the bedroom door and pauses, searching the dark hallway for danger. A siren wails from somewhere far below. The apartment is black, the air thick and dusty. The burning smell pervades, canceling all other senses.

Water. She must have water. She takes a hesitant step into the hall and starts toward the kitchen.

. . .

September 14, 5:15 a.m., I woke to my radio alarm blaring, the volume all the way up. In a fog of exhaustion, I slowly became conscious and bludgeoned the alarm into silence. When I tried to stand, my quads were screaming—too many stairs. With a groan, I got up and hobbled around the apartment, getting ready for the day. I gulped a cup of coffee along with some ibuprofen before heading back to Pier 40 for round two.

That morning was cold and rainy. It was nice to have a break from the heat, but the gloomy weather seemed to lower people's spirits even more. Everyone went about their jobs with a quiet intensity, and no one felt like making small talk. We were only able to make one run before downtown was "frozen" again, and no one was allowed in or out. I sat in my car and waited glumly for the freeze to lift, eyeing the subdued and sad-looking crowd of pet owners huddled under a tent.

My radio crackled, then I heard "Salaks, are you on the air?"

"Go ahead, Base," I answered.

"Can you come back to the office and bring some staff down to Pier 40?"

"That's a 10-4, Base, I'm en route to the A now." It was better than sitting around.

On my way uptown, I passed Bellevue Hospital. Taped to every exterior surface within reach were hundreds upon hundreds of fliers put up by families and friends of the lost. I stopped for a red light and sat staring through the rhythmic slashing of my windshield wipers as the rain poured down upon all those names and faces. Most of the writing had started to run in the heavy rain, and it gave the illusion that the whole wall was crying. So much sorrow. My own eyes blurred, and I gave in to the tears.

• • •

She wakes before dawn, still thirsty, smelling the rain. The apartment is cooler, the bad smell diminished. The rain makes her think of water, and she rises and goes cautiously into the kitchen. Last night, she had found a half-inch puddle in her dish. This morning, the dish is dry. She licks hopefully at it, tasting only metal.

• • •

I think I sat through several red lights before I got ahold of myself. I became aware of traffic easing around me in the rain. Amazingly, no one honked. If nothing else, this disaster had brought out a little more kindness, a little more patience in people.

That wasn't the only time I saw evidence of the good heartedness of people during those days. There was the doorman in a restricted zone who stayed by himself for days in a building with no power, giving food and water to the stranded pets of the evacuated tenants. I encountered supers in other buildings who did the same. There was the teenage boy with a cooler full of bottled water by the side of a Pier 40 access street. He was giving out bottles of water to any thirsty workers who happened by. He offered me a bottle one day when my throat was raw from coughing. I tried to hand him a dollar, but he pushed it back, saying, "Hey, it's cool. I don't want your money. I just appreciate what you're doing."

Countless volunteers donated food and supplies as well as their time to pass them out. Once, someone handed me a sandwich, and before I knew it seven or eight people were tossing food and drinks through my car windows. I had to chuckle as the food piled up on the seat: a banana, more sandwiches, cans of soda, snack bars, and cookies. Later, I passed the food along to a group of hungry people still waiting their turn at the pier.

Then there were the cheerleaders. These were the people who lined up day and night, in all weather, near the West Side Highway, cheering for every vehicle carrying Ground Zero workers—squad cars, ambulances, even Con Edison trucks. They held up homemade signs and posters with messages of encouragement. One I remember said, "Red, White, and Blue: These Colors Don't Run." A fire truck passed them ahead of me once, and the cheerleaders applauded and yelled, "Thank you! Thank you for all your hard work!" The weary firefighters smiled and waved back. Then, when I drove by them, I heard, "Thank you, ASPCA. Thanks for getting the animals out!" And they started clapping for me. It meant so much to all of us working down there to hear their thanks and their positive messages.

Once, I escorted a couple into their apartment to rescue their cats and a pair of gerbils. FDNY (the fire department) had checked the building for structural damage, and there were boot prints of firefighters in the dust all over the building, even in their apartment. While the couple went to round up the cats, I found the gerbils' cage and peered inside, hoping they would still be alive. Two pairs of bright and beady eyes peered curiously back at me. Then I noticed something else in the cage and had to laugh. One of the firefighters checking out the apartment must have seen the gerbils and had taken the time to throw them something to eat—it's just that his rodent recognition skills were a little off. Inside the cage was a block of New York State cheddar!

At some point, our base of operations was moved from the pier to King Street, farther downtown. Apparently, enough outside agencies had rallied at the pier to finish the rescues at Battery Park City, so we were going to concentrate on assisting pet owners in other buildings closer to Ground Zero.

We were still mostly in buildings without power, and it wasn't until the last day that I got a building with a working elevator. Once, I trudged up thirteen flights with a couple to get their cat and two turtles. When we got to the apartment, the cat was fine, but there was an awful, rotten smell coming from the turtle tank, the water was green with slime, and the two red-eared sliders were cold and motionless at the bottom.

I know that lots of people find it hard to understand how you can love a reptile, but a pet is a pet in my opinion, and you can't tell people what kind of animal they should love. This woman was really broken up over those turtles, and I felt bad for her. She stood in front of the reeking tank, her hands on the glass, and sobbed.

"Come on, honey," the man consoled her. "There's nothing we can do. Let's be thankful we got Tigger." He put his arm around her and started to lead her away from the aquarium, the cat carrier in his other hand.

Now, I happen to have a soft spot for turtles. I once owned a pair of red-eared sliders myself. I racked my brain trying to remember anything from the turtle owners' guidebook that might help. I couldn't think of a thing, but not wanting to give up hope, I told them, "Maybe they're just in shock. Let's bring them with us, and maybe the vets can do something." I didn't really believe those stiff, stinking turtles were coming out of that tank alive, but it seemed to give the woman a little hope. She quickly got a plastic bowl and plopped the turtles into some fresh water.

On the way back to King Street, I kept catching sight of her tear-streaked face in my rearview mirror. I felt bad. *If only we'd gotten there sooner,* I thought. At least we got them out. I shuddered to think what that apartment would have smelled like in another few days. Suddenly, there was a scratching sound coming from the backseat, and the woman let out a squeal. "They're moving! Oh, God, thank you, they're alive!"

Sure enough, in the fresh water and the warm car, the turtles had revived and were scrabbling around in the plastic bowl. When I dropped them off at King Street, I got a huge hug from the happy couple. I guess it might have been even better if we'd saved a cuddly little kitten, but I still smile whenever I think of that rescue. A pet is a pet.

Now, I happen to have a soft spot for turtles. I once owned a pair of red-eared sliders myself. I racked my brain trying to remember anything from the turtle owners' guidebook that might help.

One day, I was on my way back from the Javits Center carrying a load of supplies. I went through a yellow light and, just to be on the safe side, turned on my rack lights and siren. Then I noticed a yellow cab speeding toward me from behind. The cabbie was driving like a maniac, honking his horn and weaving around the traffic, getting closer and closer to me. *Oh, no,* I thought, *he's going to hit me.*

That didn't happen, but he drove up beside me, still honking. *What is this guy's problem?* I thought. I glanced over at him and saw through his open passenger window that he was trying to get my attention, gesturing frantically. It was then that I noticed something flapping around his head: it looked like a large bird.

I bleeped my siren again and pulled over, and he double-parked beside me. I lowered my window so I could talk to him. He was a neat little Indian man with a thick accent. "Oh, boy, officer, am I glad I ran into you," he said excitedly. "You have to help me. I have a bird in my cab!" He lifted his right arm, and sure enough, perched on his forearm was a great big red parrot.

He told me he had gotten out of his cab to get something from the trunk and the bird had just flown down from somewhere and landed on his shoulder. It was wearing an ID band on one leg, and a leash dangled from the other. Apparently, the bird had escaped from its owner and was lost.

"Look, I don't have any place to put him," I said. "My car is full." I gestured to the supplies stacked to the ceiling in the back of the Blazer. Even the passenger seat was loaded. "Can you follow me to our base?"

"I am sorry, officer, I cannot do that. I am already late, and Habib has this cab for the next shift. Will you please help me and take this bird?"

Reluctantly, I got out and went around to his window. I offered my arm, and the bird looked me over, then stepped quickly from the cabbie's arm to mine. The cabbie sped away, and I got gingerly back in my car, eyeing the bird, hoping he would behave. Suddenly, he grabbed my lapel and climbed to my shoulder.

"All right, bird," I warned him. "Let's not try anything cute." Apparently, he just wanted to be riding high. I drove back to King Street with a giant red parrot perched on my shoulder, acting as if he belonged there. "Oh I am a Pirate King . . . ," I sang under my breath.

Later I heard that our Adoptions department was able to trace the owner of the bird through the breeder tag around his leg. So the bird did eventually find his way home.

· · ·

She is sleeping in her corner when there is a sound that wakes her. She lifts her head, her ears keen in the silence, listening intently. Then, sure enough, she hears it: footsteps and voices. Are They coming? She scrambles to her feet and hurries to the front door, stumbling once on the way. Too many days without food and water have made her thin and clumsy. At the door she listens, quivering. People talking. Men's voices, and their heavy boots tromping down the hall. She calls out to them, a hoarse bark.

"You hear that?" one of the voices says.

"Yeah. Sounds like a dog. Poor thing. The owner musta left and never came back."

"I think it's coming from here."

They are right outside the door now. In an intense wave, she smells the burning smell on them and grows quiet. The scent terrifies her, and she backs away from the door.

"I don't hear it anymore." A kissing sound. "Here doggy. Here."

Belly down on the carpet, she listens fearfully.

"Should we go in and look for it?"

"Nah, we can't. Anyway, you got no tool. How you think you gonna break that door?"

"I'll go down to the truck and get a Halligan."

"Come on, we gotta finish checking the building. Write down the address, we'll call the ASPCA and tell 'em about it."

The footsteps and voices move away from the door, growing fainter. When she can't hear them anymore, she rests her chin on the floor and closes her eyes. She is too tired to move back to the bedroom.

• • •

For almost two weeks, the ASPCA continued to escort people into their buildings in restricted areas to rescue their pets. Of course, most people had dogs or cats, but there were also turtles, iguanas, geckos, mice, rats, gerbils, hamsters, guinea pigs, fish, rabbits, and, of course, snakes.

The snake owner I encountered looked like a twenty-something pothead surfer-dude. He'd been staying at his girl-friend's house for about a week before 9/11, so by the time we got to his apartment, his five-foot-long ball python, Austin, hadn't eaten for a couple of weeks. His building was right across from the Pile, on a block where a number of buildings had been declared unsafe. I was anxious to get in there before they closed the area completely.

"Yo, Dude," he commented when he first saw the wreckage of the towers. "That's messed up."

His living room had a giant window facing the World Trade Center site. I was amazed that it hadn't broken. He sauntered around the place, which was mostly intact, looking things over. "Cool," he said.

"All right, let's get this over with," I said, indicating that he should go ahead and feed the snake.

"Dude," he acknowledged me. He set down his backpack and pulled a plastic container from it. Inside was a mouse.

"Dude, I brought you a little snack," he said to the snake.

I won't go into the details, but after about fifteen minutes the meal was over. He grabbed his backpack and hung it over one shoulder. "OK, I'm ready. Let's go."

"What about Austin?"

"Oh, it's cool. He ate, so we can take off."

Too much pot, I thought. *Way too much.* I shook my head. "You can't leave the snake here," I said slowly, as if explaining some-thing to a toddler. "A bunch of these buildings have already been declared unsafe. Yours could be, too. If that happens, the building could be demolished." I looked hard at him to see if he was getting it. "Austin will be demolished, too," I said, so there could be no doubt.

He just shrugged. "Whatever," he said and started walking toward the door.

"Hold on," I said sternly. I put on my best officer face. "Get Austin," I ordered him. "We're not leaving until you do."

I don't really care for snakes myself. But that wasn't the point. We were supposed to be getting animals *out* of danger, not leaving them *in* danger. Plus, if he didn't care about the snake, why go through all the trouble and risk of coming down here? "Get him," I said. "I mean it."

"I can't," he said, looking pained.

"Why not?"

"Dude, it's my girlfriend. She hates snakes. She'll totally freak. I can't bring Austin to her house."

That was probably the first intelligent thing that had come out of his mouth. Now that I knew he had a few brain cells working, I just had to figure out a way to persuade him to bring the snake.

"Look. How long have you been with your girlfriend?" I asked him.

"About four months."

"And how long have you had Austin?"

"Two years."

"Dude, Austin wins. It's a no-brainer."

He gave me an uncomprehending look, so I explained. "You've had Austin for a long time, longer than you've known your girlfriend. You've bonded. He's part of you. If your girl-friend can't accept that . . . " I left the rest hanging.

> *I don't really care for snakes myself. But that wasn't the point. We were supposed to be getting animals out of danger.*

Slowly he began to smile. "Dude, you're right. Maybe it's time to find a new girlfriend."

"Oh, sure," I said. "After all, that's much easier than finding a new snake."

The sarcasm went right over his head, but I had won him over. A few minutes later, Austin was safely ensconced in a pillowcase, and we were out of there. At King Street, I found him a plastic pet carrier someone had donated that seemed reasonably snake proof.

"Cool, thanks."

"You're welcome, Dude. Good luck with your girlfriend."

"Dude," he said, with a surfer salute.

With a wave, I left him and went back to the main desk for another assignment.

• • •

She has not heard any more people in the building. The apartment is cold at night now, and sometimes during the day. Sometimes she rouses herself slowly and makes the rounds, searching the rooms: kitchen, living room, bathroom, bedroom. There is a towel on the floor there that smells of Them. She sniffs it longingly and lies down, staying near it.

• • •

Although it was uplifting reuniting pets with their owners, it was grueling for everybody to be in that environment day after day. One day, I ran into a K9 cop who had been working down at the Pile. We both had the same wheeze and hacking cough and had stopped to grab a bottle of water.

"How's it going down there?" I asked him.

He shook his head. "It's rough, let me tell you. It's rough."

"Are you guys finding anything?"

"No." He looked down for a moment. His dog, a big handsome German Shepherd Dog wearing a fluorescent orange vest, lay at his feet, waiting. "It's hard. They search all day and don't find anything. The dogs are getting depressed, you know?"

I nodded. He sounded so defeated. "You guys are doing a great job down there," I told him. "We're all behind you."

"Thanks," he said. "Good luck."

"Good luck to you, too."

He raised his water bottle in a solemn salute, and I did the same in return.

• • •

Eventually, she no longer moves from the corner. Waiting is all there is.

• • •

One day I picked up a couple whose grim, tired faces seemed familiar. Then I recognized them: it was the same couple I'd escorted down to the restricted zone that night when the National Guard stopped us. They were still waiting, desperate for another chance to try to get their dog out.

Again, we made our way down and around the convoluted route to the area where their building was. Again, we were blocked by a National Guard soldier.

"You've got to be kidding," the man said. There was an edge to his voice.

The soldier was still, except for his eyes. They shifted from me to the man and stayed there.

"Come on," I said to the couple. "Let's go."

"Oh, come on! This is ridiculous. Our dog has been up there for I don't know how long without water. We've got to get to her!" The soldier didn't even blink. The man turned to me and pleaded, "There's got to be something you can do!"

"Come on," I repeated, and turned away. "We'll try again later," I said loudly, for the soldier to hear.

"What do you mean?" the woman said. She sounded heart-broken. "I don't understand. We can't keep doing this. Why can't we just go in and get our dog out?"

I motioned for her to be quiet and follow me. "I have an idea," I explained, when we were out of earshot of the guards.

The couple followed me down the block. Let me just say, I have plenty of respect for the job the National Guard does and for the rest of our troops as well. My father was in the Air Force, and my brother was in the Navy. But the military knew nothing about the ASPCA or our operations at Ground Zero. I had given up on the Guard. They were great, but none of them were homeboys. I was looking for a New York City cop.

We walked around the barricade and saw soldier after soldier, and at last I spotted one lone NYPD officer. We were both on the home team; we were New Yorkers. He was bound to understand. Luckily for us, it worked. I quickly explained our mission to him; the cop let us through the barricade, and we were inside the restricted zone.

We hadn't gone ten feet past the barricade before the woman broke into a run. I scurried after her and grabbed her shoulder. "Stop," I warned her. "Don't run. If you attract attention, you're going to get us kicked out of here."

"She's right," the man said.

With all the restraint we could muster, we strolled to the couple's building. Fortunately, no one stopped us.

At the entrance, the woman turned to me with a look of total gratitude on her face. She grabbed both my hands. "Thank you so much," she murmured.

"You can thank me when we've gotten your dog out. What breed is she?"

"A Lab mix," she said. "Mostly yellow Lab."

"They're great dogs," I offered.

Minutes later, I was leading them in yet another climb up sixteen flights of dark and dusty stairs.

• • •

This time, she doesn't get up when she hears the sound of voices in the hall. But then there is a different sound, familiar, the key turning in the lock, and the voices, louder, Their voices. She rises, staggering, and goes toward the sound, and she doesn't need the flashlights to know it is Them. The waiting is over. They have come home.

• • •

I think the woman had the key to their door out and ready before we'd gone five steps. When we finally reached the right floor, the two of them practically sprinted to their apartment. When the door opened, we were all quiet for a few seconds, shining our lights around the dim living room.

"Stella?" the woman called, starting toward the kitchen.

The man whistled. "Come, Stella," he called.

At first we didn't hear anything. *Oh no*, I thought. *Please don't let us be too late.* Then suddenly, there was a sound from down the hall, and a young Lab came careening into the room.

"Oh, my God, Stella—she's OK, she's OK!"

She was a little thin and somewhat dehydrated. But that didn't stop Stella from doing her best to jump into the arms of her overjoyed owners and lick them to death while greeting them with the happiest sounds I've ever heard from a dog. They may not speak English, but I know for a fact that dogs can talk.

The owners were thanking me over and over, but just seeing them reunited with their dog, and seeing the happiness in that dog's big brown eyes, was thanks enough.

In the period following the collapse of the World Trade Center towers, the ASPCA rescued more than 300 pets. Usually, we're out looking for people who are mistreating their animals. What made the 9/11 rescues special was that, for a change, we were working with people who genuinely loved and cared for their pets. It was filthy, exhausting work, the hardest job I've ever done, but I'd do it again in a heartbeat. We helped so many animals and brought happiness to so many people in the face of so much sadness and grief.

Except for maybe one antisnake girlfriend.

Those Magic Moments

CHAPTER 11

L ife as a special agent is unpredictable. Forrest Gump said it best: "You never know what you're going to get." I guess every once in a while I'd have what you might call an ordinary, almost boring day—but not usually. Here are a few of the tricky, sticky, and downright icky situations I found myself in while trying to do my job for the ASPCA.

Snooping Agent, Hidden Duckling

"Here comes Peter Cottontail, hopping down the bunny trail; hippety-hoppety, Easter's on its way." Oh, those cute little Easter critters—bunnies, chickies, duckies—they're so sweet and fuzzy, and they even come in pastel colors!

According to New York State law, it is illegal to sell baby rabbits, chickens, and ducks as pets. Or to dye them, for that matter. This, however, does not stop some individuals from trying to make a few extra bucks at Easter by selling the baby birds and bunnies. It's a big problem: every year in March or April, depending on which month Easter falls in, we get calls from people reporting abandoned ducks and chicks The kids get a cute little pet in their Easter baskets, but after the colored dye wears off and the poop starts to pile up, the parents cart the little critters off to a park and leave them there to fend for themselves. The luckier ones might get dropped off at an animal shelter. Some get left on the doorsteps of pet shops. Unfortunately, unless the ASPCA actually catches someone in the act of abandoning one of the animals, there's not much the agency can do.

I was working Staten Island when I got a call that wasn't really a cruelty complaint. An anonymous caller had reported seeing a duck in a pet shop in the Dongan Hills area. I had no trouble finding the place. A kid was standing behind the counter; he looked about eighteen, a skateboarder type with longish hair and baggy clothes. I took a quick look around. There were parakeets and canaries for sale, but no ducklings— not that I expected to see them on display, if there were any. I turned to the kid.

"Is the manager here?" I asked him.

"No. I'm the only one here." He licked his lips nervously. "Can I help you?"

He already looked a little scared of me; I suspected a cover-up. I decided to jump right in before he had too much time to think about what to answer. "Do you have a duck here?" I asked, watching him closely.

"No, ah, we don't have any ducks," he said, managing to sound fairly cool and collected.

Some people are expert liars. This kid definitely needed acting classes. I decided to play along for the moment. "No ducks. OK. Well, since I'm here, I'm going to do an inspection."

"OK, whatever," he said with a shrug.

He was acting nonchalant, but I smelled a rat—or in this case, a duck. I started down one side of the store, checking out the caged animals. The kid busied himself behind the counter, pretending not to care, but several times when I glanced at him I caught him watching me.

Whenever the ASPCA gets calls on pet shops, it's routine procedure for the investigating agents to do an inspection of the place. They look at the condition of the animals and make sure the cages are clean and not overcrowded. They also check to be sure the animals have adequate food and water supplies and keep an eye out for sick animals. I had brought my clip-board with the inspection form on it and began strolling around, checking off sections on the form. This place appeared to be fairly well kept. But while I was making the rounds inspecting the cages, I kept looking for any place you might hide a baby duck. Right away, I spotted a closed door in the back of the shop. I strode purposefully to the door, my ducky senses tingling.

"Where does this door go?" I called.

The kid hurried over. "Oh, that goes down to the basement." He was looking nervous again.

"What's down there?" I asked him, although I suspected I already knew.

"Uh, it's . . . uh, it's used for storage," he stammered.

"Do you mind if I look around?" I touched the doorknob.

For a second, he looked as if he might try to stop me, but then he must have thought better of it. "OK," he said. He flipped on a light switch, and we started down into the basement, with me leading the way. At the bottom of the stairs, I paused to look around. I could see that the area was indeed used for storage: dog food, pet supplies, and—what a surprise—a fluffy yellow duckling in a cage.

"No, officer, no ducks here," I said sarcastically.

The kid stared me down for about five seconds, then his bravado wilted. "So what now?" he asked.

I wasn't really mad at him, but he hadn't been straight with me. I decided to teach him a little lesson. "Well, now you get arrested," I said nonchalantly, reaching for my handcuffs.

A look of utter panic came over him. "What? This isn't even my duck!" he protested.

"Oh, trying to pass the duck, eh?" I said with mock sternness. He was too freaked out to get the joke. I allowed him to panic for another ten seconds before I let him off the hook.

"How does it feel to be lied to?" I asked him. I watched his expression change from terrified to indignant to "caught with your hand in the cookie jar."

"Let's try this again," I said. I stuck out my hand for him to shake. "Hi, I'm Officer Salaks from the ASPCA," I said warmly.

I could see that the area was indeed used for storage: dog food, pet supplies, and— what a surprise—a fluffy yellow duckling in a cage.

His face was now bright red with embarrassment, but I think he'd learned his lesson. He shook my hand and managed a small smile. "Hi, I'm Matthew," he said.

I went on, as if we were rehearsing a scene in a play. "Hi, Matthew. I'm here because I got a call that you have a duck on the premises."

Matthew was a quick study. "Yes, officer, we do have a duck. And he's right here." He smiled as if he were showing off the grand prize on a game show and made a sweeping gesture that included the little Aflac mascot.

I smiled broadly to show him he was doing fine, and he went on to tell me the usual story: someone had left the duckling on the doorstep of the pet shop, and the shop owner had taken it in. Matthew filled out the paperwork and surrendered Baby Aflac.

The vets at the ASPCA hospital checked the duck out, declared it healthy, then oohed and ahed over its cuteness. When I left the hospital, the duck was paddling happily about in a pan of water.

Of course, as it's illegal to own farm animals in the city, it's not easy to get a duck adopted. I puzzled over where we could find a home for the little fellow. Then I had an idea. The stable where I boarded my horse already had a mixed flock of chickens, guinea fowl, ducks, and Canada geese that had found their way to the small pond on the property and never moved on. I asked the barn manager if she would mind one more, and she gave me the OK to bring Baby Aflac out to the farm. When I let the duck out of the carrier and it saw the water and the other birds, it gave a happy little quack, waddled to the pond, and jumped in.

And, yes, I had to say it: the duck stops here.

The Year of the Dog

I think one of my favorite things about New York is how many cultures you find living elbow to elbow all over the city. I love that I can be up in Washington Heights and experience the Dominican Republic one day, then another day be over at Brighton Beach getting the feel of the former Soviet Union, or down in Chinatown with its endless pulsing flow of people and energy. I've done the best I could with the two years of high school Spanish I'd had. In other cultures, I've still managed to make myself understood even when the only English they knew was "No English." Still, more than once, I wished that I were multilingual or at least a multicultural expert. It would have cut down on the misunderstandings.

Of all the calls the ASPCA gets, I'd say that reports of skinny dogs are the most common. One day, I was sent to investigate a skinny dog report in Chinatown. It's always packed down there, but on this day there was ten times the usual busyness and bustle because it was the Chinese New Year. I drove at a crawl through the narrow, crowded streets, searching for a place to park where I wouldn't be blocking the way. Red New Year decorations streamed from every available doorway, post, and ledge and swung in upside-down arches over the streets. I finally found a spot to park, then made my way up the block, feeling like a salmon struggling upstream.

The address of the dog in question was at the top of a five-floor walk-up. I trudged up the stairs, hoping I wouldn't have to leave a Notice to Comply. In these neighborhoods, that could sometimes backfire. The people are often so afraid to tangle with the law that when they get the Notice they call over and over. Or the opposite happens, and they're too afraid to call, so they don't respond at all. Occasionally, you have neighbors making trouble by ripping the notice off the door before the owner sees it.

I found the apartment and knocked, hoping the owners would be home and wondering whether I'd be able to make them understand why I was there if they didn't speak any English. As I said, my "Spanglish" is borderline, but my "Chinglish" is nonexistent.

An older Chinese man—mid-sixties, I guessed—answered my knock. When he saw a uniformed officer at his door, he looked surprised and then anxious.

Here goes, I thought. I summoned a reassuring smile and said, "Hello. I'm Officer Salaks with the ASPCA."

He continued to stare at me expectantly, a small, polite smile on his face.

"Do you speak English?" I asked hopefully.

"Yes, I speak some English," he said carefully.

With some relief, and remembering to speak slowly and clearly since I have a habit of talking too fast, I said, "I'm sorry to bother you, but do you have a dog here?"

"Yes. Why?"

I preferred to discuss these matters inside. In the hallway of an apartment building, you always get nosy neighbors sticking their heads out their doors to see what's going on. I asked the man if we could go into his apartment.

He stepped back and held the door open. "Please, come in," he said with a little nod.

Once we were out of the earshot of prying neighbors, I explained why I was there.

He seemed to understand me but looked concerned. "My dog is not skinny," the old man said. "Come look at him."

I followed him down a narrow hall festooned with red banners into a kitchen filled with flowers and platters of oranges. It smelled great.

"It smells so good in here," I told him.

"This is for the New Year," he replied, indicating the decorations and the food.

"It's the Year of the Dog, right?" He nodded, looking surprised that I knew. "I like reading about the Chinese zodiac. I guess because all the symbols are animals," I told him.

Then, speaking of animals, I spied a furry Maltese-type dog curled up in a cozy spot next to the stove. "This must be your dog," I said.

The old man nodded. "See, my dog is OK," he said.

The dog looked fine to me, but to make it official, I needed to feel his sides to check whether his ribs were sticking out too much.

"Is he friendly?" I asked. If not, I would have to have the owner hold the dog while I checked it over.

"Yes, Miko is friendly."

Miko stood and sniffed the back of my hand, then began wagging his tail. "Good boy, Miko," I said, turning a head rub into a search along his sides to feel for bones. This dog was not skinny. If anything, he was a bit overweight. I gave Miko a good scratching while I was at it, which the dog seemed to enjoy.

"So you know about Chinese zodiac. Do you know your sign?" the old man asked me, sounding like a teacher giving a pop quiz.

"Yes, I do." I stood up. "I'm a tiger." I took out my memo book and flipped it open so I could get down the information I needed to close out the complaint.

"Tiger is a good sign. They are brave and loyal," he said.

"And also furry," I joked, showing him the sleeve of my jacket, which was covered with a good amount of Miko's loose fur. "Can I get your name, sir?" I asked, pen poised.

"Is everything OK?" he asked.

"Everything is fine," I assured him. "I'm going to close out the complaint. I just need some information, Mister . . . ?" I gave him a questioning look.

"Lee," he supplied but continued eyeing my notebook with some apprehension.

I finished writing and closed my book. "Well, Mr. Lee, it was very nice to meet you and Miko," I said, shaking his hand.

This dog was not skinny. If anything, he was a bit overweight. I gave Miko a good scratching while I was at it, which the dog seemed to enjoy.

"It was nice to meet you, officer," he said.

I opened the door. "Happy New Year," I said.

"Here, this is for you," he said. He took a small red paper envelope from his pocket and pressed it into my hand. It was beautifully embellished with flowers and fancy Chinese symbols. "Happy New Year," he said, while nodding and smiling at me hopefully.

"Oh, Mr. Lee, that's all right. You don't have to give me anything," I protested, pushing the envelope back at him.

He avoided it. "This is Chinese New Year, you must take it," he insisted.

"Mr. Lee, I can't . . ."

"Tiger also very stubborn," he said sternly. "You take it."

I didn't want to offend him. "Well, OK, thank you," I said. "Happy New Year."

Later that afternoon, I was back at headquarters writing up my cases when I remembered the red envelope. One of the other agents was Asian American, so I decided to ask him about it. "Hey, Frank, what is this?"

He took the envelope and eyed me curiously. "Where did you get this?" he asked.

"I was checking out a skinny dog complaint down in Chinatown, and the guy gave me this."

"Well, the Chinese give these envelopes out for the New Year. They're supposed to bring good luck. Oh, and they have money in them."

"Money," I said uneasily.

"Did you write him up?" Frank asked.

I shook my head. "The dog was fine. I closed the complaint."

He started to laugh.

Slowly, it dawned on me. Maybe Mr. Lee hadn't understood completely that I was closing out the complaint and that he wasn't in any trouble. I remembered how he'd watched me writing in my memo book. "So it was a bribe? Oh, great!"

Frank was still chuckling. "This is customary. It's usually just a buck. Open it," he suggested.

I opened the envelope and pulled out a ten-dollar bill. I could feel the blood rush to my face. "I'll mail it back to him," I said, totally embarrassed.

"You can't do that. It would be an insult," Frank said.

I was so flustered at having been accidentally "bribed" that I went to talk to one of the higher-ups at the A about it. I explained the whole situation and the Chinese New Year and what Frank had said about it being an insult to send the money back. "What should I do with it?" I asked.

He laughed and said, "Get lunch."

Later, I did some more reading on the Chinese New Year traditions. The red envelopes are called *lai see*. It's the custom for married couples to give them to unmarried people, so Mr. Lee wasn't just watching me write in my memo book, he was also checking out my ring finger. The amount of money given is insignificant—it's the gesture that's important: it's supposed to bring luck and prosperity to both giver and recipient. I guess it worked for Mr. Lee and Miko because as far as I know, the ASPCA was never down there again. As for me, I bought lunch and a lotto ticket. I didn't win, but I enjoyed the sandwich and learned a couple of words of Chinese.

Hazard Pay

Years ago, when I worked in the theater, my fellow actors and I used to joke that what we sometimes had to go through was deserving of hazard pay. For example, once, during a production of *Annie Get Your Gun*, a red-hot casing fired from a blank gun went astray, somehow flipping over the bodice of my frilly costume and landing neatly in my cleavage. Let's just say, during that dance number my high-stepping was extra enthusiastic! Well, just as it is in the theater, when you're on the job as a special agent, no matter what the conditions, the show must go on—but there are times when you should definitely get hazard pay. I've told you about collectors, people who typically hoard piles of filthy stuff along with their umpteen animals. I've picked my way through mazes of roach- and rodent-infested junk in the houses of these people, half-expecting to discover a body. Sometimes the houses are so disgusting that the smell alone should qualify you for hazard pay. One guy I checked out had only three domestic animals—but he had acquired a whole colony of rats, since his preferred method for feeding his pets was to scatter dry dog food all over his driveway. When I pointed out that he had attracted the rats, his response was "Yeah, I guess they eat it, too."

Then there's chasing a sheep down the FDR Drive—that definitely qualifies as worthy of hazard pay. Throwing yourself in front of a runaway horse pulling a carriage also should get you hazard pay. (The people *in* the runaway carriage might qualify for it as well!) NYPD once raided a night club and found tanks full of rattlesnakes, tarantulas, and scorpions. Of course, they called the ASPCA. I shudder to think what would have happened if any of the creatures escaped during the removal. Hazard pay? You bet. Crawling under the porch of a 100-year-old house on your hands and knees to rescue a starving dog and her malnourished puppies might not earn an agent hazard pay. But crawling through all the spider webs under a 100-year-old porch on the way to the puppies—hazard pay. A misbehaving horse doesn't faze me at all, but misbehaving spiders or even well-behaved spiders for that matter—yikes!

And then, speaking of hazard pay, there was Rex. Here's a glimpse into what started as an episode of *Animal Precinct* but turned into a segment more worthy of *America's Funniest Videos*.

Rex was a male Rottweiler whose name should have been T-Rex. He'd been brought into the city animal shelter and was being held for a pending cruelty case. He had undergone surgery to remove an embedded collar and was ready to be moved to our hospital while we proceeded with the investigation. The film crew from *Animal Precinct* had been following his case and now wanted to document Rex's move to Bergh Memorial. I was the designated driver.

I checked in at NYCAC&C, where the staff introduced me to Rex. He was big even for a Rottie, and with all the stitches he looked like Frankendog. I was concerned about transporting him in the backseat of my car, but the staff assured me that Rex was really sweet and shouldn't be any trouble. One of the staff members who'd been handling him led him out to my car, and soon Rex was resting comfortably on the backseat, his leash wrapped around the passenger seat headrest. Before I drove away, I took one last look at Rex. He seemed quiet and relaxed. I put the car in gear and started for Bergh Memorial, with the film crew following behind.

It wasn't long before a FedEx truck managed to get between my squad car and the film crew, blocking their view. I knew they wanted to film the drive, so I pulled over as soon as I could. I was wearing a mic, so I let them know that I had stopped and would wait for them to catch up. I sat looking into the rearview mirror waiting for the familiar Explorer to appear with the film crew inside. They must have fallen farther behind than I thought.

Grrrrrrrrr.

At first it didn't register. I was so busy watching for the film crew that I didn't notice the sound.

Grrrrrrrrrr. GRRRRRRR! The growls got louder, and this time I noticed! But before I could react, Rex lunged from the backseat, grabbing my elbow like the canine version of the shark in *Jaws*.

I didn't wait around to see what would happen next—I thought he'd gotten loose. A few words I won't repeat flew from my mouth as I leaped out of the car and slammed the door before the dog could follow me. OK, I wasn't exactly Miss Manners at that moment. You wouldn't be either, I bet. I took a deep breath and noted that I was still alive. This was good. I also didn't seem to be gushing blood from anywhere. Also good. Immediately, panic turned to embarrassment. What kind of a wuss was I, anyway? Hadn't I been trained to handle vicious animals? *Yes but that didn't include wrestling a snarling Rottweiler with your bare hands,* a little voice in my head said. With Rex safely confined, my heart rate was slowly returning to normal. It was then that I noticed that my squad car was slowly moving away from me—I had left the car in drive!

Talk about dilemmas. The last thing I wanted to do was open that car door, but I had no choice. I ran along beside the car, opened the door, threw the gear shift lever into park, and slammed the door before Rex could come back for seconds. "Doh!" I slapped my palm against my forehead, feeling exactly like Homer Simpson.

About that time, the film crew showed up. "Oh my God, I heard the whole thing," the sound guy cried. "I thought you were getting mauled! Are you OK?"

"Yeah, I'm OK," I said. I showed them the chewed elbow of my jacket, still sporting a gob of dog saliva. "It's a good thing I was wearing my jacket."

Needless to say, I wasn't about to get back into that car. It was too dangerous. I called CACC, and the staff sent their van. Rex went quietly with the same worker who'd handled him before, and I went back to headquarters, finished my paperwork for the day, and headed home.

Talk about qualifying for hazard pay!

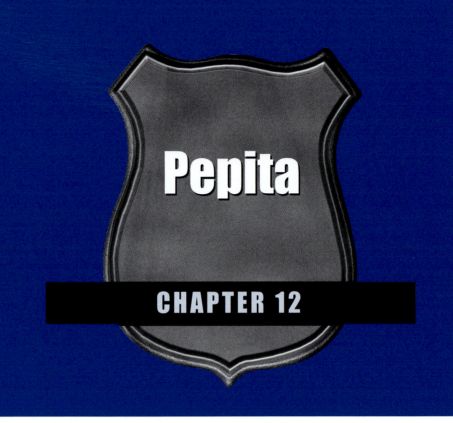

Pepita

CHAPTER 12

I had just finished checking out a case in downtown Manhattan when I got an emergency call from headquarters: "231, are you on the air?"

Now, the ASPCA uses live dispatch all the time, but back in those days, dispatch called you over the radio only if it was a real emergency. I picked up the phone and responded, knowing that whatever they were calling me about, it wouldn't be anything good.

Me: Go ahead, Base.

Base: What's your current location?

Me: Be advised, I'm in Chelsea.

Base: We have an emergency in Washington Heights. Can you handle the call?

Me: 10-4, Base.

Base: That's a 10-4. Let us know when you're prepared to copy.

Me: Stand by.

I slowed down and put on my turn signal, looking for a logical place to pull over so I could take notes. I made a quick left and double-parked on a side street, shoved the car into park, and took out my notebook and pen. I quickly jotted down what Base had already told me, then got ready to record the rest.

Me: OK, Base, proceed with the info.

Base: Caller stated that the dog was hit by a car and the owner didn't take the dog to the vet. Caller also stated that the dog is a Dalmatian and is currently in the back courtyard area. The address is 950 West 180th Street. Copy?

Me: That's a 10-4.

I was scribbling down the information as fast as I could, already thinking ahead about what I might find when I arrived at the scene.

Me: Did the complainant leave a contact number?

Base: That's a negative. Caller wanted to remain anonymous. Also be advised that we had been called out to the same address on a previous complaint. The call came in as a "Dog, no shelter," but that case was closed out as unfounded three months ago.

Me: Did we have a complainant on that call?

Base: Stand by.

The reason you check on a previous complaint is that sometimes you get the same person calling in false reports on a dog simply because it is barking or for some other annoyance, not because cruelty is involved. Headquarters would take only the basic facts when someone called, so if I could interview the complainant myself, I could compare the complainant's story with the subject's story and the circumstances I observed when I showed up at the address—sometimes all three were completely different.

Base: 231, be advised, that call also was anonymous.

Me: 10-4, Base, thanks for checking. Be advised, I'm en route. Do you have a case number for me?

Base: Case #1987.

Me: That's a copy.

Base: What's your ETA?

Me: Approximately thirty minutes.

Base: 10-4. Advise us when you arrive.

I wove through the traffic toward the FDR Drive and headed north. The address was in Washington Heights, all the way at the northern tip of Manhattan. Luckily, traffic wasn't too bad, and I made it there in close to my estimated thirty minutes.

According to the report, the dog was supposed to be in a courtyard in back of the apartment building. First, I tried the main entrance, which opened into the building lobby. I took a quick look around, but there was no access to any courtyard from there. And as far as I could tell, there was no one around to ask—not all of these big old buildings have doormen. I went back outside and walked halfway down the block, where I spied a second access to the building, an iron gate that opened

The reason you check on a previous complaint is that sometimes you get the same person calling in false reports on a dog simply because it is barking or for some other annoyance.

onto a ramp leading down. *Aha*, I thought. *This looks promising.* The gate wasn't locked, so I pushed it open and started down, hoping the ramp would lead to the courtyard. I hadn't gone far when I met a guy coming the other way. He looked to be in his fifties, and his clothes as well as his hands, face, and hair were splattered with paint.

"Can I help you?" he asked.

"Are you the super?"

"Yes."

"I'm looking for a dog that was hit by a car. Do you know anything about it?" I asked him.

He shook his head, which at first I took to mean that he didn't have any information. But then he said, "Come," and beckoned the way I'd been heading.

I followed him down the ramp, which did lead into the building's courtyard. He led me all the way through the courtyard, past a garbage area, and around to a covered walkway which appeared to be an access to an adjacent courtyard.

"She is here," he gestured.

I peered into the shadowy walkway and saw the dog. She was in there, lying on an old mattress, so at least I knew she had shelter and a comfortable place to sleep.

As my eyes adjusted to the dimness, I could see that she appeared to be a Dalmatian—mostly. She had the typical white coat with black spots, but I also noticed that she had the short stocky musculature of a pit bull, so she was probably a mix. I didn't have to ask if she was friendly—her tail was thumping the mattress as fast as she could wag it. She was also smiling.

Smiling, you ask? Yes. Along with that happily thumping tail, her lips were pulled back in a friendly grin. Ask anyone who knows the breed. Dalmatians really do smile when they're happy—although sometimes with all the teeth showing, it's mistaken for a snarl.

At first, I couldn't see any obvious sign of injury. But when the super moved closer, she got up. That's when I got a look—and a whiff—of her right hind leg. It was shocking. My adrenaline kicks in when I see something like that, bringing a wave of nausea along with it; I had to look away for a few moments. I took a couple of deep breaths, blinked hard to clear my vision, then bent down to try and get a closer look. What I was seeing looked more like a piece of raw meat than a dog's leg. I'll spare you any more details; honestly, I think it was the worst injury I've ever seen.

I took out my notebook and pen and recorded the super's name, Claudio Rodriguez, and the dog's name, Pepita. I knew this dog needed care as soon as possible, but I still had to jot down a few facts.

"Do you know who owns the dog?" I asked.

"She belonged to this guy who lived here. When he moved out, he left the dog," Claudio told me.

"How long ago was that?" I asked.

"About a year ago, I think. Maybe a little less."

"And since then, who's been taking care of the dog? Have you been feeding her?"

"We feed her." He gestured to himself. "My family, you know. My wife, she feels sorry for the dog. And a lot of the tenants, they bring her food and treats. She is very friendly, so everybody likes her."

I nodded, scribbling down the info on the dog. Clearly, she was not malnourished. If anything, she appeared to have a better than average body weight, no doubt from all the treats.

"So what happened to her leg?" I asked.

He told me he wasn't sure but that someone said she'd been hit by a car. The trauma to the leg certainly looked as if it could have resulted from that, but let's just say, bad as it was, I truly hoped it was an accident.

"When did this happen, do you know?"

He shrugged. "Yesterday, I found her like this. So I think it happened the day before, maybe. I thought maybe I should take her to the vet, but I don't know if there is one around here. And I was afraid it might cost a lot of money, that I couldn't pay for it. I didn't know what to do. But then a lady who lives in the neighborhood, she's a nurse. She came over and saw the dog. She told me it wasn't too bad, and she gave me some medicine to put on it."

He showed me a stash of Betadine and some bandages the neighbor must have given him. I could see he'd applied the medication as best he could, but it was hard to figure out what to bandage. The whole leg needed it, but it must have been so painful, the idea of trying to apply a bandage was unimaginable. I guess Claudio must have thought the same thing because the bandages were still in the box.

I never found out who the "nurse" was who triaged Pepita and decided the dog's injury wasn't too bad, but I sure hope I never have to depend on her for emergency care. That leg should have been treated right away, never mind the potential for internal injuries in a dog that was reportedly hit by a car. I told Claudio that, given the circumstances, he would be considered the dog's owner and that responsibility for her care basically fell upon him. He seemed surprised at that. I also told him that, unfortunately, he'd been misinformed about how serious the dog's injury was.

"I know you were trying to help," I said. "But this medicine is not going to be enough. Pepita's injury is very bad, and she needs to be seen by a veterinarian right away."

He began to look worried. "What should I do?"

"Do you have access to a car?" I prompted.

He nodded. "I have a van."

"Take her to Bergh Memorial," I told him. "It's the ASPCA animal hospital. It's not that far from here. I'll drive, and you can follow me there."

At this point, you may be wondering why I didn't just take the dog. Well, the law says it's the owners' responsibility to have their pets cared for by a veterinarian. So, whenever possible, you try to make sure the owner understands and takes care of the animal's needs. An agent can seize an animal only if it's clear the owner is negligent or probably guilty of cruelty. Part of the agent's job is assessing intent; so far, this appeared to be a case in which the owner had good intentions but was just uneducated about the dog's medical condition.

Claudio appeared to be listening to me, but his eyes were moving back and forth between the tail-thumping Pepita and me in my uniform. I knew where the conversation was leading.

"It's going to cost a lot of money?" he asked me.

This is usually the point in such encounters when the animal's owner begins to get evasive. Many owners start by trying to put off taking the dog, then suggest that I take the dog or suddenly remember that the real owner of the dog will be back tomorrow.

"I can't say for sure what it will cost, but Bergh Memorial is usually much less expensive than a private vet would be. They might help you out with a payment plan, if you can't pay for the whole thing." I always try to be as encouraging as possible. This guy seemed conscientious, and he really didn't look like someone with a lot of money to invest in expensive surgery on an adopted stray. You don't want to cause hardship to an owner. Nevertheless, according to the law, it was his responsibility to have the dog seen by a veterinarian. I looked at him expectantly and waited for the delay tactics.

None came.

"OK," Claudio said. He wanted to go tell his wife. I said I would stay with Pepita and told him to go ahead. My gut said he wouldn't disappear on me, and I was right. He didn't try to make any excuses or even take time to wash the paint off his face and hands. He was back in less than fifteen minutes with his wife and

No matter how courteous and friendly you try to be, there is often a built-in distrust of someone in uniform. In plenty of these cases, that goes along with the very real possibility that someone could end up in jail.

their minivan. We got the dog loaded into the back of the van and drove to Bergh Memorial, with me leading the way.

As we sped toward the hospital, I reflected on the case. In all my years at the A, I had never run across another owner who was more cooperative or acted so quickly to help an animal. This guy had cared for a stray, seemingly out of kindness, then been told when the dog got injured that by law it was his job to pay for the medical care, which might be quite costly, and he hadn't balked at all. In my book, Claudio seemed like an OK guy.

All the circumstances seemed to point to that, but you just never know. People can fool you—some seem cooperative at first, then start giving you excuses why they can't take their pet to a vet. When pressed, some will check a pet into the hospital and leave a bogus address. No matter how courteous and friendly you try to be, there is often a built-in distrust of someone in uniform. In plenty of these cases, that goes along with the very real possibility that someone could end up in jail.

I had radioed ahead so the hospital could prepare to take Pepita in as quickly as possible. When we drove up, two vet techs were waiting out front with a gurney. They transferred Pepita as gently as possible from the back of the van to the gurney and rushed her inside.

I escorted the Rodriguezes into the waiting area, and we took a seat. I spoke with the couple while we waited for some news on Pepita's condition. "Why was Pepita outside in the courtyard?" I asked. "Why wasn't she in your apartment?"

Nina Rodriguez smiled sadly. "I love dogs, but I'm allergic. If I could, I would have taken her in our home, but ..." She made a helpless gesture.

She went on to tell me that when Pepi, as she called the dog, was abandoned, they didn't have the heart to take her to the shelter because they were afraid she would be euthanized. She sounded sincere to me.

"Are you going to arrest us?" she asked, looking scared.

I wanted to reassure her, but I couldn't lie. The truth was, until we got word from the doctors on Pepita's condition, this was still a cruelty case. As much as I wanted to believe that the Rodriguezes were good people and that they were telling the truth, I simply couldn't be sure until I had more information.

"Let's not worry about that right now," I told her. "We need to wait and see what happens to the dog."

Just then, she was called over to discuss payment for Pepita's treatment. It was going to be expensive. I spoke with the hospital administration and asked if we could put her on a payment plan, and they promised to look into it. I said good-bye to Nina and Claudio and went upstairs to HLE headquarters.

My boss wanted an update, so I filled him in on what I had learned so far. My gut still said this wasn't going to turn out to be a cruelty case, but I would need some interviews from neighbors who might be able to fill me in on the details of what kind of life Pepita actually had and what had really happened to her leg. So the next day, I went back to the address in Washington Heights to try to piece together more information.

What I ultimately discovered was this: On the day she was injured, Pepita had been in the courtyard. Apparently she saw a cat outside. She ran out of the courtyard after the cat directly into the street, where she was hit by a car. Probably the driver couldn't help hitting her, but witnesses said whoever it was hadn't stopped. Pepita came limping home. The Heights being a close-knit community and Pepi being something of a neighborhood pet, word quickly spread that the dog had been injured. A little later that day, the nurse who lived nearby saw Pepita and brought over the bandages and Betadine for her.

When I had finished my interviews with neighbors and witnesses, I went to the Rodriguezes' apartment and knocked on the door. I wanted to give them an update on Pepita's condition. I informed them that although she had an infection and was still on an IV, the doctors had done everything they could for her. They were hopeful that she would pull through and that she would not lose the leg.

Nina and Claudio seemed genuinely glad to hear that Pepita was expected to recover. I still felt that this wasn't a cruelty case, but I had to present the latest information to my boss. And the bill for Pepita's care was going to be substantial. We talked it over and made our decision.

The next day, I again met with Nina Rodriguez. I gave her the latest update on Pepi's condition and told her that she and Claudio would not be charged with animal cruelty. She was relieved and very grateful. Then I gave her the bad news: the bill. It was going to put a huge strain on the family, even if they made payments, and it was still growing.

"I know it's probably much more than you expected," I said gently. "I talked it over with my boss, and he thinks you might be better off signing the dog over to us."

She seemed hesitant. With a pained look on her face, she said, "I don't want to give her away. We love her, but I don't know how we can afford ...?" She gave me a sad and searching look. "If I sign her over to you, what will happen to her? Will you ...?" She broke off, waiting for my reply. I quickly reassured her that the hospital would continue to care for Pepita as long as she needed it and that when the dog was healthy again, Pepita would be put up for adoption.

"She'll stay there until someone adopts her, I promise. However long it takes."

The pained look turned to relief, and she agreed to let us take Pepita. I gave her the paperwork to sign. "You're doing the best you can for Pepi," I told her.

"I hope she will be all right," Nina said, handing me the papers. "Please take good care of her."

"We will," I promised and said good-bye.

I'm glad Pepita wasn't abused, but the injury to her hind leg was still severe, and she endured a lot of pain and a long and tedious recovery. But through it all, she remained the same tail-wagging, smiling dog I'd met that first day in the courtyard.

I figured that once the leg healed she'd be adopted quickly, as cute and personable as she was. Boy, was I wrong.

Some dogs get adopted in a few days, most in a few weeks. Pepita had been in Adoptions for over a month. Every week when I made my rounds, checking on the animals I had seen placed there, I'd go by Pepita's cage, hoping she'd be gone, adopted. But every week, I was greeted by that chunky tail-thumping spotted dog. I couldn't help feeling responsible for the pets I seized that ended up in Adoptions, especially one like Pepita, who had endured so much pain and was still so sweet and friendly. So I put on my matchmaker hat and told everyone I knew about Pepi, what a great dog she was, how cute and people-loving, how good-natured she'd remained through the ordeal of treating her mangled leg. But no matter how I spread the word and willed someone to take her, no one did.

I was having the same concerns about Pepita that I'd had about Lucky—some dogs who have never been kept in a cage will crack under the pressure of spending so much time alone and in "prison." These dogs go cage crazy, or kennel crazy—that is, they undergo a drastic change in disposition, often becoming depressed or even angry and aggressive. Of course, there are lots of people, both staff and volunteers, who come in and play with the dogs, groom them, keep them socialized, and take them out for walks and runs, but it's not always enough. If an animal becomes too hostile, there's no choice; it has to be euthanized. Poor Pepita had been through so much already; I just hoped and prayed that that wouldn't happen to her.

The months went by. Pepita had been in Adoptions far longer than any of the rest of "my" dogs. I began to wonder

> *The dog went from being "Pepi from the 'hood'" to "Pepita, Lady of Leisure." The last photo I got from her new owner was Pepita lolling by the swimming pool—and yes, I swear, she had a smile on her face.*

about the decision my boss and I had made, suggesting that Pepita's owners sign her over to us. It was this very thought going through my head over and over one day when I went to check on Pepi. I walked up to her cage and—she wasn't there. Fearing the worst, I went to the staff and asked if she was being walked or weighed or what. They told me no, then the good news: someone had finally offered a home to Pepita. I was overjoyed.

Here's how it happened: A woman who had lived in New York for many years and just recently moved to Arizona had seen Pepita's picture on the ASPCA Adoptions Web site. When she was a kid, this woman's family had had a Dalmatian, so when she saw Pepita's picture it was love at first sight. She booked a weekend trip to New York, adopted Pepita, and flew her back to her new house in Arizona. The dog went from being "Pepi from the 'hood'" to "Pepita, Lady of Leisure." The last photo I got from her new owner was a picture of Pepita lolling by the swimming pool—and yes, I swear, she had a smile on her face.

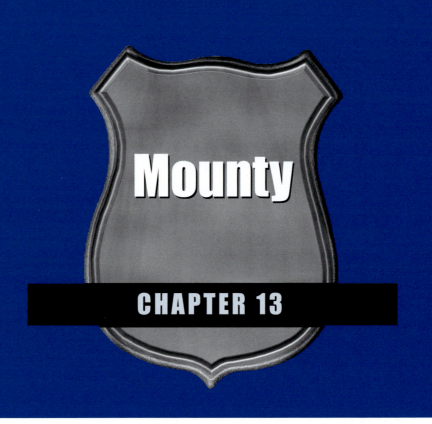

Mounty

L ife has dealt me plenty of bites, kicks, and scratches — and most of them have nothing to do with the animals I've worked with. But I guess I've had my share of the good stuff, too—like my horse. The kids at the barn call him Thunder because of the sound you hear before you see him galloping toward you from the far end of the paddock. His real name is Mounty. It would be impossible to tell how I got him without telling how I came to New York in the first place and how I ended up working as a special agent for the ASPCA. It took me a while to figure out that my path in life is working with animals, but Mounty brought me part of the way down that path. So the story of how I came to own Mounty is really the story of who I am.

When I was a kid, the thing I wanted most in the world was a horse. Not a pony—a horse. He would be a big black Thoroughbred, and I would name him Sundance. I would keep him in a stable in my backyard, and every morning I would go out to feed him and brush his shiny black coat and comb his long flowing mane and tail. Then I would ride him around our neighborhood, galloping through yards and jumping over fences. At the end of the day, we would come home, where I would feed him and brush him again. Then we would stand together under the stars, just Sundance and me, until I had to go in to supper.

I think I begged for a horse every Christmas and birthday for about ten years, besides pestering my parents between holidays. As soon as I was old enough to babysit and do odd jobs, I started saving every dollar I earned to help pay for my horse. My family had a succession of other animals—dogs, cats, birds, turtles, fish, gerbils—but no horse. I think I was in high school when it finally sank in that a horse was never going to be able to live in my suburban Milwaukee backyard. Reluctantly, I put that dream aside, but it only made me more determined to fulfill my other dream: living in New York City. Just like a dog sniffing out a buried bone, I was determined to find my way to the city.

It wasn't easy. The horse fund was barely enough for a plane ticket, and with four younger brothers and sisters, plus my mother's poor health, I knew I couldn't count on my parents to help me out. When I got old enough to get a real job, I worked after school, weekends, and summers. I took whatever I could get: waitress, salesperson, cashier, receptionist, security guard, bank teller. For a while, I even worked at a stable grooming horses and mucking out stalls.

While I was saving up to move to New York, I was also wondering what I was going to do when I got there. I wasn't sure, but I thought maybe I would be an actress. In the twelfth grade, I auditioned for a part in the school play and got cast, but my mother wouldn't let me take the part because I'd have to quit my job as a cashier to make all the rehearsals.

"You made a commitment when you took that job, and you're not going to miss all that work just to act in some play," she told me.

I pointed out that I had also made a commitment to be in the school play, but that didn't seem to matter.

The summer after I graduated from high school, I got laid off from my job at Harley Davidson. I was moodily flipping through the Help Wanted section of the *Milwaukee Journal* when the ad jumped out at me: a summer theater was hiring apprentices. I just about knocked over my chair getting to the phone to call and managed to get myself hired.

The winners of Donald Trump's show *The Apprentice* got $250,000. My weekly paycheck as a summer stock apprentice was 10,000 times less. (For those of you who hate math, that's $25 a week.) I was putting in about sixty hours a week, with only one day off every two weeks, but I didn't care. I loved it. My friends thought I was nuts, my parents hit the ceiling, and my boyfriend told me to choose—the theater or him. It took me

I was moodily flipping through the Help Wanted section of the Milwaukee Journal when the ad jumped out at me: a summer theater was hiring apprentices.

about ten seconds to choose between them; it was the single life in the theater for me.

Best of all, I finally had a reason to make the move to New York—that was where you went to be an actor. The apprenticeship was the most fun I'd ever had at work, but after two seasons of summer stock and one year at the University of Wisconsin, I thought I'd had enough training. I decided it was time to poop or get off the curb. So I took my meager savings and headed for New York.

My first job in the Big Apple—being a nanny to five-year-old twin boys—lasted just four months. I love kids, but I think that animals are much easier to work with! Broke and jobless, I had to tuck my tail between my legs and go back home. It was at this time that my younger sister Tami was killed in a car accident.

As horrible as Tami's death was for my family and me, I'd hate to think that grief is stronger than life. Although I miss her, I'm grateful for the nearly eighteen years I shared with her, and

I've learned that losing a loved one doesn't have to wreck your life. Whenever I come face to face with tragedy, I think of my sister, and somewhere I find the strength to quietly deal with it. I'd like to think that strength comes from Tami.

Things were tough at home after that. My parents reacted the way many people do when they can't handle their grief; they withdrew. We all fell into a tense cycle of numbly going to work and going to sleep and going to work again. So when a friend invited me to stay with her in California, I jumped at the chance. That lasted about six weeks, and then my dad called to say that my mom had been hospitalized for her addiction to painkillers, and he needed me to come home and help take care of my younger brothers.

I lived at home for about a year before I managed to get back to New York. I sublet an apartment with a friend and started looking for work in the theater. Six weeks later, however, my friend announced that she'd had enough of the city and left. I couldn't afford the rent, so, whipped once again, I headed back to Milwaukee.

The third time I moved to New York City, I really dug in my claws!

Some friends of mine were nice enough to let me stay with them for the dreaded "until I can get my own place," but this time luck was with me. My second day in the city, I found a job working in a pharmacy. Almost as quickly, I found my way back to the theater as a technical assistant, then began moonlighting as a production assistant on movie crews. The money was great, and I was learning a lot about the stage and the screen, but somehow it didn't feel right. I loved living in New York, but

I had this nagging feeling that theater wasn't the career for me after all.

Sometimes events in your life come together in mysterious ways. Although I'd decided working on movie crews wasn't for me, it was a movie, *The Prince of Tides*, that gave me my eureka moment and a kick back toward my first love—horses. There's a scene in the movie picturing mounted officers from the New York City Parks Enforcement Patrol (PEP). *That's it!* I thought.

Two months later, I was one of those peace officers. I was sure I had found my dream job: working with horses in New York City. Then I met Mounty.

I was a rookie officer just out of remount training, and I had been assigned to Central Park. At the time, we had three horses stabled at Claremont Riding Academy, two blocks from the park. One was Edgerton, a sturdy little chestnut who was virtually bombproof, as they say in the horse business. Sinn Fein, or "Shinny" as he was affectionately known, was a large gray saddlebred, also quite steady. Then there was Mounty, the problem child.

The captain had sent Mounty to Manhattan for additional training, and boy did he need it. He was a Belgian draft cross, which basically meant that he was as big as he was crazy. The other officers had all told me horror stories about him. He had a terrible rearing problem. Once he'd actually flipped over backward into the bed of a pickup truck. Recently, he had bucked off the officer riding him and come galloping back through the streets to Claremont. I remember thinking, *Why do we even have this horse?* My first month in the unit I wasn't allowed to ride him—as if I wanted to!

He was a Belgian draft cross, which basi-cally meant that he was as big as he was crazy. The other officers had all told me horror stories about him.

I will always remember the first time I went out on patrol into Central Park's North Woods. The park is spectacular. In the middle of one of the biggest cities in the United States, I felt as if I were back in the woods of Wisconsin. I was riding Edgerton, and my partner, Rob, was riding Mounty. It was one of those gorgeous, perfect spring days, and I was just following Rob, enjoying the sunshine and my first day out on the job. Then we came to a bridge.

There are several of these scattered throughout the park: wooden bridges over ditches, ravines, and streams, most no more than ten feet long. Rob walked Mounty up to the first crossing, and Mounty froze. Rob urged him on, and he started to rear. On the most basic level, a horse is supposed to obey the rider when asked to go forward. Mounty was doing his best to go backward, sideways, up—any way but forward. After a tense few minutes with no success, Rob suggested that I lead, and Mounty followed Edgerton over the bridge. This happened a few more times, and I remember thinking, *This is no good. What if we have to split up? Or worse, what if we have to respond to an emergency on the radio? What are we going to do, take the long way through the park because Mounty won't cross a bridge?*

A few months later, I was on patrol with another officer, Lori. This time I was riding Sinn Fein, and Lori was on Mounty. We were in the North Woods again, and surprise, surprise, Mounty was up to his same old tricks. We came to a bridge, and Mounty reared like a mad horse when asked to walk across it. He was even worse than before. I told Lori about the last time, how he would follow another horse but wouldn't lead.

"Well, he's got to learn," Lori said.

What happened next reminded me of pro wrestling's World Wide Entertainment SmackDown. Mounty would shy and snort and sidestep, but somehow Lori would get him close to the bridge. Then Mounty would rear and spin around to get away from the bridge, and the dance would begin all over again. After fifteen minutes, there was still no clear winner.

In a situation like this, it's never a good idea to let the horse think he's winning, but it wasn't looking good for the humans, and Lori was getting tired. To this day, I still can't believe the words came out of my mouth just then, but somehow they did.

"What if I got on him?"

Lori was shaking her head. "I don't think that's a good idea."

I was just a rookie officer, and she was much more experienced. I knew she was looking out for me. But I also knew that so far nothing was working and that we needed to keep trying. "Look, you know we can't let him get away with this. Like you said, he's got to learn. Let me try—I can't make it any worse, right?" I joked.

Reluctantly, Lori dismounted and handed over the reins. She held Shinny while I climbed on Mounty. What was I thinking? The horse was almost seventeen hands high and as bad as he was big. My riding experience added up to a handful of lessons when I was a kid, a year and a half of biweekly lessons and leasing a horse at a barn outside the city, and my training for the mounted unit—plenty of technical stuff, but only weeks of saddle time. *This horse is probably going to kill me,* I thought.

I don't think I was actually breathing when I turned Mounty around and asked him to square up facing the bridge. I felt as if I were in a dream as I asked him to walk. All I could hear was my own heart thumping and Mounty's huge hooves crunching the leaves underfoot. To this day I don't know why, but the horse stepped forward when I asked him to and marched right across that bridge!

Once safely on the other side, I took a deep breath and gave Mounty a big pat on the neck. It was all I could do to keep from hugging him—boy, did that feel great! "Good boy," I told him enthusiastically.

"All right!" Lori yelled from the other side. "I can't believe you got him to cross it!"

I was grinning from ear to ear. "It was just luck," I said. "He must have finally gotten tired of fighting."

"No," Lori said, leading Sinn Fein over the bridge, "I think he likes you."

Not long after that, we were told that the captain wanted horses assigned to one officer, instead of rotating among the officers. "How do you feel about taking Mounty?" the sergeant asked me.

I hesitated. It wasn't as if officers were lining up to get him. Then I thought of that day at the bridge. Maybe I had just been lucky, but there was one way to find out.

"I don't mind," I told the sergeant. And that's what started my long-term relationship with one very big, very crazy, and very lovable horse.

I didn't know anything about Mounty's background except that he came from a horse auction in Connecticut where many horses are sold for slaughter. (To this day, the thought that he might have ended up that way gives me the chills.) Whatever training he'd had was a mystery. We were starting from scratch. But the one thing I did know was that, just like people, horses crave stability. I soon realized that a lot of Mounty's bad behavior came from his insecurities. He was always being asked to face new situations with different riders who all had different styles of riding. It must have been very confusing and frightening for him.

Although the rearing wasn't his only problem, it was by far the most dangerous. After a while, I learned that certain things were more likely to set him off, so I could avoid some of them. I also learned to sense when he was about to go up—he'd slow down, and I could feel his back start to tense up, so I knew to keep him moving forward. Still, if I had a dollar for every time he reared with me . . . ! I quickly learned to lean forward and hang on, and luckily, he never got me off. I kept looking for ways to make him feel more comfortable with his job as he made me better at mine.

By the summer, I had been working with Mounty for several months. It was time for the annual police horse competition at Coney Island, and our unit was going to compete. I was nervous and excited at the same time. This was my big chance to see if all my hard work had paid off.

The day before the show, Lori and I were busy getting the horses ready. We had been brushing and clipping, bathing and braiding for hours. I was leading Mounty out of the wash stall when he spied a wheelbarrow full of grain and decided to grab a snack. Somehow, while I was wrestling him away from the grain, he managed to plant one of his gigantic steel-shod hooves firmly on top of my foot.

"Ouch!" I yelped, and tried to shove him off me. But he was too busy gobbling grain to pay me any mind, and I was too close to him to get any leverage. It seemed as if his whole 1,600 pounds was concentrated on my foot. I thought I could feel the bones crunching under his enormous weight.

"Get OFF," I yelled. Finally, he took a step sideways, and I was able to get my foot free. Cautiously, I tried standing on it and gasped. The pain was excruciating.

Lori had just noticed the commotion. "What happened?" she asked.

"Got stepped on," I mumbled. I hobbled to Mounty's head and started tugging on his halter.

Lori took the lead line and with a firm tug got him away from the feed and into his stall.

"Thanks," I said sheepishly. I sat down on a nearby hay bale.

"Let's see it," Lori demanded.

I eased off my boot, trying not to wince. The foot was already swelling, and a horseshoe-shaped bruise was starting on my instep.

I was leading Mounty out of the wash stall when he spied a wheelbarrow full of grain and decided to grab a snack. Somehow, while I was wrestling him away from the grain, he managed to plant one of his gigantic steel-shod hooves firmly on top of my foot.

"All right, let's get you to the doctor."

"No, it'll be fine," I said. "It's just bruised."

"This looks bad," she said. "You're going."

"No," I protested. "If I go to the doctor, he'll tell me not to ride, and there's no way I'm missing this horse show after all the work we've put in." I pulled my sock back on. "I'll be fine."

I promised I would go to the doctor as soon as the show was over, and Lori reluctantly agreed.

The next day, my foot was about twice its normal size and turning a deep purple. Luckily, we wore field boots with laces in the front. It hurt like heck, but by loosening the laces all the way, I managed to squeeze my foot into the boot. That was hard, but it was even harder trying not to let on that I was injured. If the sergeant had seen me limping, I would have been out of the competition in a heartbeat—or hoofbeat.

The show attracted mounted officers from all over the East Coast and even from Toronto. The Canadians were the favorites. They looked sharp, rode well, and were incredibly friendly. But we still wanted to beat them!

I was entered in three events, but the obstacle course, which each officer would try to get through as quickly as possible, was going to be the most difficult and challenging.

There were fifteen obstacles, designed to test the horse in situations he might encounter while on duty, to see how well he performed. Among other challenges, Mounty and I picked up a sixty-pound dummy and moved it to a different location. We also had to step on a board that tipped like a seesaw and, of course, cross a bridge. Mounty was perfect. I came out of the ring beaming. Of course, many other teams were just as good as we were. I knew we probably wouldn't win anything, but the ride was enough of a reward. Mounty had come a long way from that spooky horse who wouldn't step onto the bridge. When the results of the class were announced over the loudspeaker, I couldn't believe it—we'd come in second!

My partner handed me a beautiful red ribbon, and the captain came over to congratulate us. "You did really well for the short amount of time you've been with us. You should really be pleased," she told me.

Who won, you're asking? The Canadians, of course! Mounty and I also got a yellow third place ribbon that day.

After the competition, I did get my foot x-rayed. Nothing was broken, and I soon made a complete recovery. Mounty and I went on to compete in other police horse competitions, including the Police Olympics, and won lots of ribbons, even a blue ribbon and a trophy. But I'll never forget the red ribbon that was Mounty's first, and mine.

It was fall again when the sergeant asked for volunteers to work the Macy's Thanksgiving Day Parade. I jumped at the chance. It's always been one of my favorite events, ever since I was a kid. But when I told my superiors that I wanted to ride Mounty, they laughed me out of the office. "Mounty doesn't do parades," they told me. So I was assigned Edgerton.

The day of the parade was chilly and cloudy, just the way Thanksgiving should be. I admit I was a little nervous as we waited to take our places in the parade. Between the balloons and the bands and the people lining the streets, I began to think maybe I had been crazy to think Mounty would have behaved in all this. Feeling doubtful, but determined not to let it show, I lined up with the other officers, and riding boot to boot, we set off down the avenue.

Edgerton trooped along like an old pro, and I began to relax. We waved to little kids, showed off the Mounted Parks Enforcement division, and had a great time. On the way home, we left the streets and rode up the bridle path toward Claremont, letting the horses have a nice long canter to blow off some steam. It was one of the best rides I've ever had, but I couldn't help thinking, *Mounty could have done this. He would've been fine.*

So the next year, when they asked for volunteers to work the parade, I stepped up again. But this time, I was determined to ride Mounty. After all, I argued, last year there was nothing that would have spooked him. And now he had another whole year of training behind him. He was used to crowds now, and

But this time, I was determined to ride Mounty. After all, I argued, last year there was nothing that would have spooked him.

even loud street noises rarely bothered him anymore. We'd be fine, right?

Wrong.

Here is a note to the directors of parades everywhere: horses cannot be put just anywhere in the lineup. That year, we were sandwiched between a very large, very loud marching band and a giant Garfield balloon. It was a windy day—remember the year the Bart Simpson balloon almost wiped out several spectators?—Garfield was swaying and dipping constantly. Every so often, the big cat would swoop down toward us, and the horses would freeze, then begin backing up, perhaps hoping to sneak away from the monster. Then the band would start up behind us, and the horses would rush forward, startled by the sudden noise, only to be stopped again by the swooping, swaying balloon. It was pure torture. After about half an hour of this, Mounty had reached his limit. All his good manners went out the window. He started rearing like the Lone Ranger's horse, sometimes staying up for fifteen or twenty seconds, even walking on his hind legs!

All I could do was hang on and hope he got tired. This was going to be a long day. At some point, I noticed the oohs and ahs from the crowd. And it wasn't because of Garfield—they thought Mounty's performance was part of the act!

Somehow we survived that ride, and the next year, I must admit, I did not volunteer to work the parade.

I spent four terrific years with the Parks Department. By that time, Mounty and I were like an old married couple. I knew him better than I knew my best friends, and I like to think he was just as comfortable with me. I'm proud to say, by that time he had become so calm that they used him to train the rookie officers. But in spite of my attachment to Mounty, once again, after some soul searching, I had decided that it was time to move on. But to what? Working in the mounted unit was my dream job, or so I'd thought. What else could I do in Manhattan that would enable me to make a living and still work with the animals I loved?

Again, it was horses that gave me a push in the right direction. I ran into an acquaintance at the National Horse Show in Madison Square Garden. It was he who suggested that I look into working for the ASPCA. That's when the lightbulb really went on for me—since moving to New York, and while patrolling Central Park when I worked for the Parks Department, I had spotted many stray, injured, starving, or abandoned animals. I can't tell you how many times I wished I were off duty so I could rescue them. If I worked for the ASPCA, it would be my job to help them.

Three months later, having earned my badge and my "blues" (the dark blue uniforms special agents wear on duty), I suited up and went out on my first case to investigate a report of animal cruelty for the ASPCA. At the end of the day, I headed home, worn out but smiling. I knew had found my second dream job.

Working for the ASPCA would turn out to be wonderful. Leaving Mounty was something else. My last day with Parks, I went into his stall to say good-bye. I hugged his neck, tears streaming down my cheeks. "I'll miss you, Mou," I told him. He rested his huge head on my shoulder and let out a long low snort, as if to say "I'll miss you, too, kid."

About two years later, I got a call from an old friend who had also worked for PEP. She'd heard that Mounty was being retired because his allergies had gotten so bad that he could no longer work. The Parks Department thought they had found him a home, but that fell through, and they were looking for someone to adopt him.

When I got the call, I was heading out the door for a weekend getaway. I was just getting back on my feet financially and still paying back loans I'd taken out to cover my living expenses while I was between jobs. And I lived on the upper west side of Manhattan. I needed a horse like I needed a hole in the head. But having longed for a horse my entire life, I thought this was fate. And I felt responsible for Mounty. What if he ended up some place where nobody cared about him? What if he ended up at one of those livestock auctions again, the kind where the dog food buyers go?

I canceled my trip and started making phone calls. With a lot of help from my friends, I soon became the poor but proud owner of a 1,600-pound bouncing baby boy!

The only place I found where I could afford to board a horse was over an hour from the city, at a stable in New Jersey. To visit Mounty, I had to borrow a friend's car or take a train and a bus for nearly four hours roundtrip. Still, I did my best to get out there every week on one of my days off. Knowing how Mounty hated changes in his routine, I was worried that he might not adjust to being retired and living in a strange new place. As it turned out, I didn't need to worry. He quickly took to his new surroundings and made friends with the other horses he was turned out with. Even better, with all the fresh air, and by switching from straw bedding to shavings, he was soon able to stop taking his allergy medications.

In spite of his large size, Mounty was known to be very gentle. One day, the owner of the stable approached me. She ran a riding program for the handicapped and wanted to know if I would consider lending them Mounty. She had a new kid in the program, a big teenage boy, and all of her horses were too small for him. I said she could give it a try, and it turned out to be a perfect match. Since I was letting them use my horse, they stopped charging me board, and I didn't have to worry that Mounty wasn't getting enough exercise.

Things went on smoothly for a while. Sharing Mounty with the handicap program was great for everybody, and I came out as often as I could to take my horse for a ride. Strolling through the woods near the stable or cantering down one of the trails, I couldn't help feeling that I was blessed to be the owner of such a magnificent animal. Mounty seemed to be as happy as I was.

It's always a phone call that pops the balloon. In the spring of 2002, the barn manager called to say that Mounty was colicking. In horses, as in humans, colic means a bad belly-ache. But in horses, the problem is serious and can even result in death. I rushed out to the barn. The vet had seen Mounty by then, and he was up and looking pretty well. When treated early, these things usually turn out OK, so I went home with my fingers crossed, hoping that the worst was over.

Two days later, I got another call. Mounty was down with the colic again, and this time it was worse. I spent a tense day by his side as my friend Scott, a former vet tech, helped me change bags of saline solution on the IV drip the vet had set up. Mounty received more than fifty liters of fluid. By the end of the day, he was up again and starting to nibble his hay. Then he passed manure, always a good sign, and we breathed a sigh of relief. This time, it seemed, he really was going to be all right.

Again, two days had passed when the owner of the stable called to tell me that Mounty had relapsed. The news was grim. After so much stress on his large but delicate digestive system, Mounty was dying. There was a chance that with surgery they could save him, but it was a very small chance, and the surgery would cost thousands of dollars. "He's suffering now," she told me. "It's bad. You have to decide if you want to put him through the surgery or go ahead and put him down."

I've never felt so helpless. I knew every second was impor-tant, but I needed a minute to think. "I'll call you back," I told her, wishing I was by Mounty's side instead of sixty miles away.

I felt as if I'd been punched in the stomach. Poor Mounty. After all that he'd been through, it just didn't seem right that he should have this painful end to his life. I didn't have the $7,000 to pay for the surgery, and there was no way I could take out

After so much stress on his large but delicate digestive system, Mounty was dying. There was a chance that with surgery they could save him, but it was a very small chance, and the surgery would cost thousands of dollars.

any more loans. Even if I could afford it, the surgery was risky, and the recovery would be long and slow—if he recovered. I couldn't stand the thought of Mounty suffering. The kindest thing would be to put him down, before the pain got any worse. Struggling to keep back the tears, I reached for the phone and dialed the stable.

"Hello?"

"It's Tina," I said.

"What do you want to do?"

As if in a dream, I started to tell her my decision. Then I stopped myself. When I investigated complaints, I was always telling people to take their pets to the vet. I had waited all my life to own a horse. How could I just end his life with a phone call, without trying everything possible to save him?

"Tell them to do the surgery," I said. "I'll get out there as fast as I can."

"Are you sure that's what you want to do?"

I thought of Mounty refusing to cross that bridge all those years ago and the joy I'd felt when he finally did it for me. This would be one more bridge for us to cross, but maybe, just maybe, we would make it over this one, too. I had to hope.

"Yes," I said. "I'm sure."

The ride to the New Bolton Center for large animal care in Kennett Square, Pennsylvania, seemed to last forever. All the way there, my hands were shaking, and I had a dull ache in my stomach. What if it was already too late? What if Mounty died before they could even start the surgery?

When we arrived, I quickly explained to the veterinarians how Mounty had been sick off and on for several days. They were surprised that he had survived this long. Most horses in his condition don't last more than two or three days.

While they prepped Mounty for surgery, I filled out the paperwork. A vet pulled me aside before they took Mounty in and asked for my consent to euthanize Mounty if, once they opened him up, it turned out that there was no way to help him. Fighting to hold back the tears, I said yes, at the same time praying that it wouldn't come to that. Then I gave my horse one last hug before he went into the operating room, knowing it might be the last time. "Just one more bridge, Mounty," I whispered to him.

Then there was nothing for me to do but go back to the center's barn and wait. Before I left, I asked the doctors what Mounty's chances were. They said about 25 percent. They wouldn't know exactly what was causing Mounty's colic until they opened him up. Then, if they could find the problem, there was no guarantee they could correct it. His intestines might already be too damaged from all the stress. If they did find the problem and fix it, and if he survived the surgery, the next hurdle would be preventing a massive infection. Mounty was an older horse, and his system was already weak from his being sick for so many days. It didn't look good.

In spite of the low odds and the huge expense, I still felt that I owed it to my horse to at least try. I could always make more money, but there would never be another Mounty.

Back at the stable, I collapsed on the beat-up couch in the office and tried to rest. As exhausted as I was, I couldn't sleep. But as more and more time passed, and the phone didn't ring, the more hopeful I became that at least Mounty would survive the surgery.

At dawn, the phone finally rang. Mounty had made it through the surgery! He had an impacted cecum, which is a small pocket in the intestine where partly digested food can collect. The doctors did a bypass and removed the damaged section of the intestine. They cautioned me that Mounty wasn't out of the woods yet and that the next twenty-four hours would be crucial. The biggest problem now was preventing an infection.

Still, I was overjoyed. I took the bus back to the city and went straight to work, bleary eyed but relieved. I knew how stubborn Mounty was. If he'd fought this long, I knew he wasn't going to quit.

Mounty proved me right. When I saw him a couple of days later, he was so thin I almost didn't recognize him. He was weak and moving slowly after all he'd been through, but there was a look of clear calmness in his eyes, and I knew he was going to

> *He was weak and moving slowly after all he'd been through, but there was a look of clear calmness in his eyes, and I knew he was going to be all right.*

be all right. After ten days, he was discharged and sent back to the stable to recuperate.

When it was all over with, I had more than $9,000 in medical bills for Mounty. The stable owners generously paid the barn vet bill, and my parents and my sister helped me make a down payment on the balance. The New Bolton Center let me make payments, which I'm still paying off, but I don't mind. It's sort of like that credit card commercial says:

Fee for adopting your horse: $250

Medical expenses for emergency colic surgery: $9,000

Having your horse recover and hearing his twenty-one-year-old hooves thundering toward you across the pasture for a carrot: priceless.

• • •

Here we go with the Oscars, but I can't help it. I'd like to thank every single person at the New Bolton Center, from the dedicated assistants to the brilliant doctors—you guys are the best. If I ever win the lottery, I'm planning to make a huge donation, and maybe you can name the new wing after Mounty.

Thanks to my family and friends who supported me both emotionally and financially through the whole ordeal. And a special thanks to everyone at the barn who took care of Mounty while he was recovering, including the grooms and every barn rat who helped hand walk Mounty four times a day. Thank you from Mounty and me from the bottoms of our hearts.

About the Authors

ALLISON ESTES is the author of more than fifteen books for children and adults, including *The Short Stirrup Club* series and various titles in the YA series *Thoroughbred*. She also works as an editor and teaches writing classes through the New York Writers Workshop, of which she is a founding member. For eighteen years, she was a trainer at Claremont Riding Academy in Manhattan. She is originally from Oxford, Mississippi, but has lived in New York for more than twenty years. She has a grown daughter and a young son, and she plays softball as much as possible.

TINA SALAKS is a former Special Agent with the ASPCA's Humane Law Enforcement Division in New York City, where she investigated animal cruelty complaints for seven and a half years. Some readers may remember Tina from Animal Planet's TV show Animal Precinct, where she was a regular for five seasons. Before she joined the ASPCA, Tina was a mounted officer with the New York City Parks Department, and Tina adopted her horse Mounty after she left. Tina grew up in Wisconsin and has lived in New York City for twenty years. This is Tina's first book. She still supports animal causes, and she is hoping to adopt another horse.